John Holt:
personalised learning instead of 'uninvited teaching'

by Roland Meighan

Educational Heretics Press

Published 2002 by Educational Heretics Press
113 Arundel Drive, Bramcote Hills, Nottingham NG9 3FQ

British Library Cataloguing in Publication Data

Meighan, Roland
John Holt: personalised learning instead of 'uninvited teaching'
I. Title
370.92

ISBN   1-900219-23-9

Design and production: Educational Heretics Press

Cover drawing of John Holt by Annabel Toogood

Printed by Mastaprint Plus, Sandiacre, Nottinghamshire

Contents

**Educational Heretics Press
exists to question
the dogmas of education in general,
and schooling in particular.**

Introduction

In this second edition, I have corrected the title of the first edition, *John Holt: personalsied eduction and the reconstruction of schooling*, for in the end, John Holt did not hold that schooling could be rescued but needed to be phased out or just scrapped, and replaced with arrangements for learning that were more intelligent, and not based on 'uninvited teaching'.

In John Holt's ten books there are just a few biographical asides, but for the most part he stays with the task of developing ideas about education. He mentions two sisters, Jane Pitcher and Susan Bontecou. We learn that he did not marry but he says that this was not of his choosing - things just did not work out for him that way. He was born in 1923 in New York City and died of cancer in September 1985 in Boston. The British Press did not note his death or his contribution to education because the regressive, fascist-tendency in education that John Holt described as on the march in USA, was already in fashion amongst politicians, civil servants and the media in England.

He spent a few years in the navy, where he says he learnt a great deal about co-operation in the confined spaces of submarines. Later he worked in Europe in the world government movement. When he returned to USA, he took up work as a teacher in private schools. It was in such schools, amongst the wealthy and 'successful', that he began to develop his ideas about how children fail and how schooling destroys both the intelligence and spirit of children.

In the last phase of his life, he set up *Holt Associates* to further the causes of educational change and reconstruction. He supported the development of the home-schooling movement in USA by founding *the Growing Without Schooling* magazine and support group.

A passer-by saw a copy of a John Holt book on the Educational Heretics Press bookstall. *"I see that John Holt is still at work,"* he said. I corrected him: *"Sadly, he died in 1985."* *"I know,"* the passer-by said. He leaned over and picked up the book for me to see. *"But he is still at work!"*

One of my hopes in writing this review of John Holt's ten books is that it will help ensure that John Holt goes on working.

Roland Meighan
June 2002

How Children Fail

When my first partner came home from her school clutching a copy of *How Children Fail,* in 1965, as I recall, I was not to know where this incident would lead. Shirley was a teacher of the younger children at one of the few Primary schools in the Midlands ever to try to take the Plowden Report ideas at all seriously, much to the incredulity of the other schools in the area. Wherever the 'Plowden revolution' was later alleged to have taken place, I can report with some confidence that it was **not** in the Midlands since I and my colleagues were in and out of the region's primary schools with our students on a regular basis. Indeed, the research such as the ORACLE project from the University of Leicester, indicates that it hardly took place anywhere, despite the assertions of mis-informed tabloid journalists based on a few anecdotes - some rare but true, others rare and only partly true, and others invented.

The head teacher had asked all the teachers on the staff to read *How Children Fail* in preparation for a staff meeting to reflect on the work of the school in the light of John Holt's ideas. So Shirley read it and then I read it and then we faced up to it: what Holt had to say squared uncomfortably with our experience.

The central message was stark: **most children fail in school and indeed, the model on which we set up school, could hardly do anything else.** Most fail in the school and society defined tasks of first learning the imposed curriculum and then passing the tests derived from it. That was a grim verdict in itself, although not a new one. John Holt went further and pointed to a deeper sense of failure:

> *"... they fail to develop more than a tiny part of the tremendous capacity for learning, understanding, and creating with which they were born and of which they made full use during the first two or three years of their lives." (p9)*

Holt proposed that school, in collusion with the dominant parts of the culture in which it operated, actually **reduced** the intelligence of most children so that they came out after 15,000 hours or so of schooling less intelligent than when they went in. In *How Children Fail,* Holt was concerned to show how he had come to this conclusion and, more importantly, his observations in classrooms that attempted to uncover the underlying mechanisms, or in the current educational new-speak, 'the delivery systems'.

How to make schools worse

There is a terrible irony in re-reading John Holt's message. Most of the bad strategies he identified that were fostered in the private schools, in which he taught and did his observations and analysis, are those which raise children's fears, and produce learning which is fragmented, distorted and short-lived. They have become the basic building blocks of the UK National Curriculum. Consequently, school has been made even worse. The same process was evident in the last few years of Holt's life in the USA and he contemplated writing a book entitled *How to Make Schools Worse* to document the regressive developments as they occurred. He founded the organisation *Growing Without Schooling* instead, as we shall see in a later chapter..

He also demonstrated the failure of the ideas of the 'progressives' about making school work better:

> *"They thought, or at least talked and wrote as if they thought, that there were good and bad ways to coerce children (the bad ones mean, harsh, cruel, the good ones gentle, persuasive, subtle, kindly), and that if they avoided the bad and stuck to the good they would do no harm." (p175)*

As an example, he looked at the New Maths and was unimpressed. What he saw was the old maths rearranged in a different pattern. It was still cook-bookery maths even if some of the recipes looked newer and more inviting. Holt proposed that children cannot learn much of any use from 'cookbooks', new or old, because they do not learn effectively by trying to transplant someone else's reality into their own, but by building up their own reality from the experiences they encounter. This was how young children learned and why they were such prolific and successful learners, a theme Holt took up in his last book, *Learning All the Time.*

A second irony is that Holt has been labelled as a 'progressive' himself and identified with the very ideas he sought to expose. There was, he maintained, no way to coerce children without making them afraid, or more afraid. Fear is the inescapable companion of coercion and its inescapable consequence. We must reject, therefore, the idea of schools and classrooms as places where, most of the time, children are doing what adults tell them to do, if we are serious about **educating** them rather than **schooling** them.

The questions Holt set out to answer were these:

"How does this mass failure take place? What really goes on in the classroom? What are these children who fail, doing? What goes on in their heads? Why don't they make more use of their capacity?" (p10)

His method began as a series of memos written in the evenings to a colleague and friend whose fifth grade class he both observed and taught in during the day. Later he arranged these memos under four main headings that reflected the themes that had emerged during his observations. They were Strategy; Fear and Failure; Real Learning; and How Schools Fail.

Holt taught in private schools with reputations for high standards and he was at pains to point out that his book was not about 'bad' schools or 'backward' children, indeed, almost the reverse. Parents were paying out good money to have their children attend these schools. To all outward appearances the schools and the children were successful. The harmful effects of the schooling in question were given a blind eye, not least because they were somewhat subtle in their operation:

*"**Strategy** deals with the ways in which children try to meet, or dodge, the demands that adults make on them in school. **Fear and Failure** deals with the interaction in children of fear and failure and the effect of this on strategy and learning. **Real Learning** deals with the difference between what the children appear to know or are expected to know, and what they really know. **How Schools Fail** analyses the ways in which schools foster bad strategies, raise children's fears, produce learning which is usually fragmented, distorted and short-lived, and generally fail to meet the real needs of children." (p10)*

Strategies in classrooms

There were various strategies that emerged from Holt's observations. Some resist any involvement at all because they do not want the embarrassment of making mistakes and learn to avoid it. Others attempt to find tricks to locate the right answer. They are the 'producers' who focus on feeding their teachers the right answers they signal that they so clearly prize above all else. They jump at right answers and if they fail they fall back into despair or defeat. It does double harm if they do get right answers by their strategies:

"When a child gets right answers by illegitimate means, and gets credit for knowing what he doesn't know, it does double

*harm. First, he doesn't learn, his confusions are not cleared
up; secondly, he comes to believe that a combination of
bluffing, guessing, mind reading, snatching at clues, and getting
answers from other people is what he is supposed to do at
school; that this is what school is all about; that nothing else is
possible." (p.146)*

Others try to please the teacher, whether they have any clue as to the right
answer or not, by waving hands in the air enthusiastically - provided at least
six others, including some successful 'producers', have their hands in the air
too. A common strategy, Holt noted, was mumbling answers, for a teacher
anxious to get a right answer will assume that anything that sounds close is
meant to be the right answer. An associated strategy is 'guess and look':

*"There was a good deal of the tried-and-true strategy of **guess-
and-look**, in which you start to say a word, all the while
scrutinising the teacher's face to see whether you are on the
right track or not. With most teachers no further strategies are
needed." (p.29)*

A few children are 'thinkers' who try to assess meaning and work for
understanding despite the dominance of the right answer culture. They are not
helped by teachers who have such a fixed idea of the answer they require that
they dismiss answers offered which are logical or even alternative correct
answers. The culture of right answerism had another unhelpful tendency,
which was to value the 'yes' and other positive answers more than the 'no' and
negative ones even when the information yielded was the same:

*"This, of course, is the result of their miseducation, in which
'right answers' are the only ones that pay off. They have not
learned how to learn from a mistake, or even that learning from
mistakes is possible. If they say, 'Is the number between 5,000
and 10,000?' and I say yes, they cheer; if I say no, they groan,
even though they get exactly the same amount of information in
either case." (p. 46)*

Relief often followed a mistake, for correct answers create a strain and anxiety
because more right answers are then expected. The consequence is a low
tolerance of uncertainty in both teachers and taught as answer-grabbing and
teacher- pleasing take continual precedence over thinking and understanding.

Holt concludes that the results of all this are far from trivial. The strategies are *defensive* in attempting to avoid trouble, disapproval, loss of status, embarrassment, ridicule and other punishment. They are *fear-laden and neurotic*. They are *self-limiting and self-defeating*. In the process children's intelligence is destroyed and their behaviour becomes more and more stress-laden. They are learning to behave stupidly in the school's terms in its 'temple of right answerism', with the 'teacher high-priests' devoted to the doctrine of 'tell them and test them'. Only the few determined 'thinkers' can ride out this system and survive intact.

Teacher versus pupil interpretations of intelligent behaviour in schools

But from the children's point of view, their behaviour is intelligent because it minimises stress. They give up on thinking school will ever make any sense. The point is to survive each day with as much dignity intact as possible:

> *"For children the central business of school is not learning, whatever this vague word means, it is getting these daily tasks done, or at least out of the way, with a minimum of effort and unpleasantness." (p.37)*

But this approach neither serves them well in the pursuit of the school's desires, nor does it develop their confidence as learners with understanding. Furthermore, it does not match the teacher's idea of taking the students on a journey to some glorious destination well worth the pains of the trip;

> *"So the valiant and resolute band of travellers I thought I was leading towards a much-hoped-for destination turned out instead to be much more like convicts in a chain gang, forced under threat of punishment to move along a rough path leading nobody knew where, and down which they could hardly see more than a few steps ahead. School feels like this to children: it is a place where **they** make you go and where **they** tell you to do things and where **they** try to make your life unpleasant if you don't do them or don't do them right." (p.37)*

Tests just make things worse

These false messages about learning are reinforced by tests. Tests are supposed to make children work harder. Holt disagreed. Since children tend to feel threatened by tests, they work worse not better. Scared soldiers might be thought to fight better, but a scared learner is almost always a poor learner.

Tests are supposed to show what children have learned. But teachers everywhere need good test results, as much, if not even more than children to prove that they are 'good' teachers. So tests are announced in advance and the type of contents outlined. Practising and coaching in the kind of material to appear in the tests then follows. Students recognise the dishonesty of stressing and rewarding this shallow appearance of knowledge rather than working for real, deep understanding:

> *"In short, our 'Tell-'em and test-'em' way of teaching leaves most students increasingly confused, aware that their academic success rests on shaky foundations, and convinced that school is mainly a place where you follow meaningless procedures to get meaningless answers to meaningless questions." (p. 151)*

Why children fail

From his research, John Holt provided three answers to the question of why children fail. They fail because they are afraid, or bored, or confused. These often occur in combination.

> *"They are afraid, above all else, of failing, of disappointing or displeasing the many anxious adults around them, whose limitless hopes and expectations for them hang over their heads like a cloud.*

> *"They are bored because the things they are given and told to do in school are so trivial, so dull, and make such limited and narrow demands on the wide spectrum of their intelligence, capabilities, and talents.*

> *"They are confused because most of the torrent of words that pours over them in school makes little or no sense. It often flatly contradicts other things they have been told, and hardly ever has any relation to what they already know - to the rough model of reality that they carry around in their heads." (p10)*

How Children Learn

People sometimes express disappointment on reading John Holt's second book after the provocative nature of the first. Part of the reason may be the switch from the challenging emphasis of the first book, to the steadier and slower task of beginning some reconstruction in the second.

In *How Children Fail,* Holt described children using their minds badly, induced by the standard school regime to use their minds, not to learn, but to get out of doing the things imposed on them by adults. In the short run these strategies work and it makes it possible for children to get through their schooling even though they learn very little in the process. In the long term, the result is far from trivial: it is the destruction of effective intelligence so that children are prevented from growing into more than limited versions of the confident, courageous and effective learners they might have become.

In *How Children Learn,* the task Holt set himself was to explore those situations in which children use their minds well, learning boldly and effectively. Most of the examples to be found were of children learning before starting school:

> *"In short, children have a style of learning that fits their condition, and which they use naturally and well until we train them out of it. We like to say that we send children to school to teach them to think. What we do, all too often, is to teach them to think badly, to give up a natural and powerful way of thinking in favour of a method that does not work well for them and that we rarely use ourselves." (p.7)*

A different vision of school was possible. If we have a better understanding of how children learn, Holt proposed, we could reconstruct schools so that they became places where all children grew, not just in size, but in curiosity, confidence, courage, independence, resourcefulness, resilience, patience and competence.

Some features of effective learning were already known but largely ignored. Firstly, we know that vivid, vital, pleasurable experiences are the easiest to remember. Secondly, we know that memory works best when unforced and that 'it is not a mule that can be made to walk by beating it'.

We also know that we think badly and even perceive badly, when we are afraid, anxious or under stress. These are the situations in which we say 'we are just not thinking straight at the moment'. In Holt's view, this describes the emotional atmosphere of most classrooms most of the time.

These two enterprises of understanding better how children learn, and then re-constructing schools in the light of these understandings, would take some time:

> "To find out how best to do this will take us a long time. We may find, in fifty or a hundred years, that all of what we think of as our most up-to-date notions about school, teaching and learning are either completely inadequate or outright mistaken." (p.8)

These tasks also required the exercise of caution, what Bertrand Russell called constructive doubt and others have seen as the sceptical approach:

> "There's an old story about two men on a train. One of them seeing some naked-looking sheep in a field, said, 'those sheep have just been sheared'. The other looked a moment longer, and then said, 'they seem to be - on this side'. It is in such a cautious spirit that we should say whatever we have to say about the workings of the mind, and it is in this spirit that I have tried to write, and in which I hope others will read, this book." (p.9)

The book is divided into five main sections followed by a concluding chapter. The five sections are *Games and Experiments, Talk, Reading, Sports*, and *Art, Maths* and *Other Things*. Each section contains observations of children in learning situations and Holt's interpretations of the events. His intention, Holt states, is to locate and describe effective learning more than to explain it.

Lisa, aged sixteen months, is the subject of several of the observations in the first section on Games and Experiments. Her work, which adults might call play, is accompanied by pseudo-speech she has invented. She fits screws and other small objects neatly into their holes and this makes him wonder if the clumsiness of small children is overstated. Holt's typewriter provided other opportunities for investigation and her actions with the machine became more refined and controlled by both practice and imitation. The piecing together of cause and effect is a constant part of Lisa's work:

> *"This morning Lisa bent down to pick up a balloon and, as she did, a puff of wind coming through the door blew the balloon across the floor. She watched it go. When it stopped, she moved close to it, and blew at it, as if to make it go further. This surprised me. Can such young children make a connection between the ability of the wind to move objects, and their own ability to move them by blowing on them? Apparently they can."*
> *(p. 15)*

Because we tend to underestimate children, we can easily overlook the nature of what they are doing. Lisa walks round the balloon singing but she changes her song and then changes it again until it is a different song altogether. A musician might call it variations on a theme. Singing is usually encouraged in the first encounters with school, Holt notes, but they all sing the same songs taught by the teacher who often aims to 'get them right' not to make up something new. Uniformity takes over from improvisation.

Small children are self-motivated, Holt observes, but school sets about substituting external motivation and then worrying about why it this so ineffective:

> *"It is not hard to feel that there must be something very wrong with much of what we do in school, if we feel the need to worry so much about what many people call 'motivation'. A child has no stronger desire than to make sense of the world, to move freely in it, to do the things he sees the bigger people doing."*
> *(p.17)*

He muses that good presents for young children might be eggbeaters, flashlights or saucepans. If they get broken, it costs little. Later thousands of pounds will be spend on trying to get children learning, so begrudging the cost of a few household objects is a false economy.

From his observations, Holt proposes that games are a prolific source of learning. Spontaneous games often begin by accident. The spirit behind them is sometimes joy, sometimes foolishness, at other times exuberance but they all involve finding out how the world works. So, education might be regarded as a huge game, 'the game of trying to find out how the world works'.

> *"Recently Lisa has started to play fierce games. She bares her teeth, growls, roars, rushes at me. I pretend to be afraid, and cower behind a chair. It can go on for some time. From this, and many other things she does, it seems as if she feels a* Me *inside her growing stronger, doing things, demanding things. Any game that makes* Me *seem more powerful must be a good game. Most of the time she knows all too well how powerless that* Me *is. ... Children don't mind letting us the adults win the game, as long as we let them score a few points. But so many of us, like some football coaches, seem never to be content with merely winning; we have to run up the big score." (p. 20-1)*

Throughout the book, John Holt's stories about children learning are used to reflect and draw out some ideas about effective learning. From observing Lisa, he notes a series of points. She does not feel she has to get everything right before starting but is willing to begin by doing something and then modifying it. Next she was not satisfied with incorrect imitations but kept looking and comparing until she was satisfied she had got it correct.

Lisa coped well with uncertainty. She hears things all day that currently make no sense to her, but she doesn't appear to mind: *"She lives in uncertainty as naturally and easily as a fish lives in water." (p.23)* When do children begin to crave certainty?

How do they catch this and many other fears from others? Thus, Lisa never seemed to be afraid of bugs, but after she witnessed someone else screaming because of the presence of a spider, she has been wary, draws away from all insects and doesn't want to watch them. Part of her curiosity about the world has been killed off.

Yet when Lisa is interested in something, her patience and concentration can be astonishing. Her learning is an end in itself and she is not doing it to please an adult or gain someone's approval. A mother writes to John Holt and seems to throw some light on this. She says of her son that he hates to be taught but loves to learn things. Is learning in order to please adults and submission to unwanted teaching something that will be caught later in the competitive and status-conscious situations of a nursery school?

Holt concludes this section by commenting on the *apparent* inefficiency of children's learning. They often pile up a lot of raw sensory data before trying to sort it and make sense of it. Until this has happened, they may have no clear ideas about what questions they are going to start asking. Adults would usually move much more quickly into imposing a pattern, almost any pattern, to cope with their inability to tolerate confusion and uncertainty. But the child's method is superior in situations that are new and confusing, and this is typical of many real-life situations, and it prevents them from coming to hasty and erroneous conclusions on the basis of too little evidence. Most schooling discourages this approach which is then doomed to become stunted and then destroyed.

In the second section Holt proposes that the most difficult thing we ever learn is to talk. It takes very subtle and complicated co-ordination of lips, tongue, teeth, palate, jaws, cheeks, voice and breath. So, how is it learnt? The answer appears to be patient and persistent experiment, by carefully comparing the results of these experiments with the speech of the other people around, and by not being afraid to get things wrong before setting about correcting them.

There is a contrast between this natural, effective method of learning and the stilted, ineffective methods schools usually seek to put in its place. The remark that, if we tried to 'teach' children to talk, they would never learn it, is used to speculate how a committee of experts would set about devising a talking curriculum. There would be lists of speech skills, words, syllables and sounds. There would be plenty of drill, review and tests. Holt forecasts that most children would become baffled, discouraged, humiliated and fearful and would give up trying to learn to talk.

Lisa grew up on a cattle ranch and so it was no surprise that at eighteen months she was pointing at cattle and saying *"See cows, see cows"*. A few days later she said the same thing to a field with some horses in it and later to a field of sheep. We did not correct her. She had apparently isolated a class that we would call 'large animals in fields' and had identified them as cows. By listening to others talking she realised that there were sub-groups to her classification and learned to put the conventional name on each one. The adults around were allowing her powers of self-correction to operate and her confidence in being able to work it out.

> *"A child's understanding of the world is uncertain and tentative. If we question him too much or too sharply, we are more likely to weaken that understanding than strengthen it. His understanding will grow faster if we can make ourselves have faith in it and leave it alone." (p. 65)*

In any case, classifying is not just a matter of sorting words but of complex understandings such as that a similarity is a difference that does not make any difference. Thus, although chairs may differ in details, they are all essentially the same. 'Telling the answer' looks like a helpful thing to do and sometimes it is, especially when asked a question, but letting children work it out encourages their thinking strategies.

The adult anxiety to get it right immediately can be counter-productive. Holt cites Patrick, who at two years of age, could not pronounce S, Z, SH, CH, or any other sibilant sounds. 'Spoon' came out as 'Poon'. Nobody fretted and before long he had put the matter right by himself. But supposing the adults had been correcting him every time he spoke? He might have just got discouraged and reticent, or he may have developed a stutter or a stammer, since research has shown this is at least one way that stutters develop.

This approach always upsets some people. After meetings where John Holt was speaking, he often received letters challenging him on this point. One psychologist asserted that we should correct all the mistakes that children made. Holt wrote explaining further how counter-productive this can be, but to no avail. Evidence was not the issue, he concluded, but belief in the indispensability of experts. Anyone who makes it their life's work to help others can fall into the trap of believing that the 'clients' cannot really get along without them and reject any evidence that they are frequently capable of standing on their own feet.

> *"Many people seem to have built their lives around the notion that they are in some way indispensable to children, and to question this is to attack the very centre of their being." (p.69)*

Children who start to talk, however, are taking a bold leap into the world. Anyone who has tried to use a foreign language in another country experiences the same thing. You are encouraged if the native speaker tolerates your halting attempts to use the unfamiliar words, but discouraged if you encounter one who insists on 'teaching' you the correct grammar and the perfect pronunciation. Holt recounts his own experiences in trying to speak Italian when he spent a year in Italy where he encountered many helpful and patient Italians.

> *"A child learning to talk needs the kind of curious, attentive, sympathetic audience that I found in Italy. At first, he is not sure that this language business really works. Even after many years of talking, he may not feel that he can get his most important thought and feelings across to other people." (p. 71)*

In Italy this tact is extended to children, but this is not necessarily so elsewhere. It seems, Holt observes, to be a rule in USA and UK that you should be tactful with other adults and not insistently to point out their speech errors, but this courtesy is not automatically extended to children. It is no surprise, therefore, that children do not particularly like to hear stories about their younger days. What seems cute to adults, is a reminder to children of their littleness, helplessness and clumsiness. Childhood is not a blessed, romantic state of bliss, but a state of powerlessness and something to escape from as quickly as possible and then to be largely forgotten. This became the theme of his later, and perhaps his most radical book, *Escape From Childhood.*

Classrooms do not necessarily help children become better at talking. Lack of conversation is likely to lead to poor readers and poor writers later.

> *"Bill Hull once said to me, 'Who needs the most practice talking in school? Who gets the most?' Exactly. The children need it, the teacher gets it. ... The result of this kind of education is that children of ten or even older may be no better at talking than they were at five."*

Holt did not see the 'progressive' ideas as much of an improvement. He did not see the so-called revolution of the 1960s as altering things much since the stilted question and answer sessions and the brief fake discussion and conversation interludes were little or no improvement on telling and lecturing. No real increased practice in talking took place.

In the third section the theme explored is that of reading. Many of the observations made about talk are now applied here. Again, the stress is on giving children support whilst they learn to figure it out and avoiding actions that emphasise their limited competence.

Holt notes that children often learn well from slightly older children. One reason may be that the older child understands the language of the younger and can speak in their terms. But another is that the gap in competence is not so forbidding - the older child is more within reach than the adults. Adults who can read well can easily forget the problems of de-coding print. One way to remind ourselves is to try to make sense of an unfamiliar script.

> *"One day I took a sheet of printing in some Indian language, and tried to find the words that occurred most often on the page. It was amazingly difficult. At first the page looked like nothing but a jumble of strange shapes. Even when I was concentrating on one short, common word, it took a long time before I could recognise that word at sight and pick it out of the others. Often I would go right by without noticing it." (p.91)*

In the same way, he concludes, it takes children time to get used to the shapes of letters and if they come from homes where reading is less prevalent, they will need to go through this familiarisation stage in the classroom. Again, the self-checking and self-correcting skills should be allowed to operate and rushing in to correct mistakes too soon or too often, only serves to extinguish these skills.

> *"What we must remember about this ability of children to become aware of mistakes, to find and correct them, is that it takes time to work, and that under pressure and anxiety, it does not work at all." (p.94)*

One source of pressure is the timetable. Holt expresses his exasperation with this kind of thinking about learning:

> *"Timetables! We act as if children were railroad trains running on a schedule. The railroad man figures that if his train is going to get to Chicago at a certain time, then it must arrive on time at every stop along the route. If it is ten minutes late getting into a station, he begins to worry. In the same way, we say that if children are going to know so much when they go to college, then they have to know this at the end of this grade, and that at the end of that grade. If the child does not arrive at*

*one of these intermediate stations when we think he should, we
instantly assume that he is going to be late at the finish. But
children are not railroad trains. They don't learn at an even
rate. They learn in spurts, and the more interested they are in
learning, the faster these spurts are likely to be." (p.100)*

In a short section on learning and sports, most of the observations are drawn
from young children learning to swim. He notes the developing interest and
confidence of the infant Tommy as he is taken regularly to the pool. His
progress in exploring was uneven. His courage to try new things rose and fell
like the tide. The baby in the pool had moments of courage and exploration
and then times of retreat and retrenchment. Tommy sometimes let John tow
him around in the water kicking his feet and paddling with his hands but then
he would revert to wanting to hold on to him tight or be held tight.

Other parents would try to teach their infants to swim without getting very far
because they were not sensitive enough to this rise and fall of courage. They
could end up with a counter-productive experience. One parent succeeded in
reducing all three of his children to tears and terror in this way.

*"If we continually try to force a child to do what he is afraid to
do, he will become more timid, and will use his brains and
energy, not to explore the unknown, but to find ways to avoid
the pressure we put on him." (p. 111)*

In the section on *Art, Maths* and *Other Things*, the research of David Hawkins
on learning science is invoked. Hawkins found that when he made it a rule
that children have a period of completely free play with the materials before
going on to any directed work, the quality of the learning increased. Hawkins
proposed that we have to cross the line between ignorance and insight several
times before we truly understand and that dragging or shoving us across does
not do all that much good. A theme that Holt develops in his later books
begins here, that teachers may teach but that learning does not necessarily
follow.

*"We teachers like to think that we can transplant our own
mental models into the minds of children by means of
explanations. It can't be done." (p. 143)*

From his careful observations of children, John Holt sees it differently. Children see the world as a whole, even if it is a mysterious whole. They make their own paths into the unknown often using routes we may not have anticipated. When they learn this way, following their curiosity, children go faster and cover more territory.

In the final section, *The Mind at Work*, the strands of the earlier observations are pulled together. Holt reflects on how children seemed better able to solve a commercial puzzle than he could and decided it is because he tried to reason about the puzzle far too soon, whereas children explored the pieces thoroughly and experimented with them randomly. With this thorough awareness of what the pieces were like and what they could do, they could then start to apply reason to the solution. This was not an attack on the value of analytical, deductive, logical reasoning. Detectives, scientists and car mechanics make great use of it. But it needs to be kept in its appropriate place, and it is less useful in education than we are led to believe. Teachers are encouraged to accept an 'astonishing delusion'. They are pressed to believe in the magic power of explanation.

> *"We think we can take a picture, a structure, a working model of something, constructed in our minds out of long experience and familiarity, and by turning that model into a string of words, transplant it whole into the mind of someone else."* (p.164)

Although this sometimes works, it is not all that often and most of the time explaining does not increase understanding all that much, and may even lessen it. Holt recognises that this conclusion makes defenders of the system angry. They say we have to teach the children symbols because human knowledge is stored that way. They do not recognise that teaching the symbols, i.e. explaining them in words, does not produce any more than shallow understanding at best.

> *"They have to make the journey from reality to symbol many times, before they are ready to go the other way ... But when we do what we do most of the time in school - beginning with meaningless symbols and statements, and trying to fill them with meaning by way of explanations, we only convince most children either that all symbols are meaningless or that they are too stupid to get meaning from them."* (p. 166)

The natural learning style of children impresses John Holt. Because they are curious and want to make sense out of the world, gain competence and control over themselves and their surroundings, they are experimental, open, receptive and perceptive. They do not sit back and observe the world, but taste it, feel it, touch it, push and pull it, and generally explore it. They are bold - in spasms - and not afraid to make mistakes and learn from them. They do not have to have instant meaning but can be patient whilst meaning emerges.

In contrast, school is a place in which, after initially supporting this style, less and less time, opportunity or reward is given for this kind of thinking and learning. Instead it sets about gradually undermining confidence in this approach and replacing it with something far less effective which is ultimately counter-productive by turning most children off learning altogether. Holt states his belief that we *can* devise schools that get back to the effectiveness of natural learning.

> *"What is essential to realise is that children learn independently, not in bunches; that they learn out of interest and curiosity, not to please or appease the adults in power; and that they ought to be in control of their own learning, deciding for themselves what they want to learn and how they want to learn it." (p.169)*

Two objections are commonly raised against this proposal. The first is that this implies that children have to re-invent the whole culture for themselves. It is the word 'discover' that creates the problem here. The whole culture is out there already invented but the method of learning about it being proposed is first-hand and not third-hand by accepting the second-hand verbal accounts of others.

The second is the 'essential knowledge' belief. Holt sees this idea as full of fallacies. People cannot agree what this essential knowledge consists of. Therefore, it is no surprise to find that the various National Curriculum offerings around the world differ astonishingly in their contents.

Next, there appears to be no knowledge that is essential for everyone that they will not encounter anyway. This was how they absorbed the essential bits of knowledge needed to master the skills of talking.

Then knowledge changes so rapidly that what was seen as essential one year simply becomes fallacious or redundant later.

> *"Believers in essential knowledge decreed that when I was in school I should study physics and chemistry ... Of my chemistry, I remember only two or three formulas and a concept called 'valence'. I mentioned valence to a chemist the other day and he laughed. When I asked what was so funny, he said, 'Nobody talks about valence any more; it's an outmoded concept'. But the rate of discovery being what it is, the likelihood that what children learn today will be out of date in twenty years is much **greater** than it was when I was a student." (p.170-1)*

Observing young children learning leads John Holt to propose that they are natural learners, that birds fly, fish swim, and humans learn and think.

> *"Therefore, we do not need to 'motivate' children into learning, by wheedling, bribing or bullying. We do not need to keep picking away at their minds to make sure they are learning. What we need to do, and all we need to do, is bring as much of the world into the school and the classroom; give children as much help and guidance as they need and ask for; listen respectfully when they feel like talking; and then get out of the way. We can trust them to do the rest." (p.172)*

The Underachieving School

John Holt's third book is a collection of sixteen short pieces and many of them appeared as articles in pamphlets, magazines or books. Acknowledgements are given to *Harper's Magazine, Life, New York Review of Books, New York Times Magazine, The PTA Magazine, Redbook,* and *Yale Alumni Magazine.* In the foreword, John Holt notes that his thinking about education was undergoing change and that the essays reflect this.

The first essay, *True Learning*, signals his growing unease about schooling. His starting point is that education is not what someone gives or does to someone else, but something people do for themselves. He points to a mismatch between the learner's needs and the school experience that is imposed:

> *"What young people need and want to get from their education is: one, a greater understanding of the world around them; two, a greater development of themselves; three, a chance to find their work, that is, a way in which they may use their own unique tastes and talents to grapple with the real problems of the world around them and to serve the cause of humanity." (p.13)*

Society also requires three things: that the traditions and higher values of the culture be passed on, along with a general acquaintance of the world in which we are living, and thirdly, some preparation for employment. All these tasks used to be undertaken by the family in the community, until mass schooling was adopted. Schools, however, are proving to be inadequate to the task:

> *"None of them is done well by schools. None of them can or ought to be done by the schools solely or exclusively. One reason the schools are in trouble is that they have been given too many functions that are not properly or exclusively theirs." (p.13)*

Schools, therefore, should be a resource from which people can take what they need in the activity of educating themselves. Given that there is an infinite number of roads to education, each learner should be free to find and devise his or her own.

A short essay, *A Little Learning*, deals with some reservations about Piaget's theory of learning and the nature of the experiments on which it was based. These were rather confused in nature, Holt contends, and they relied too much on the idea that thinking in its highest form is mostly the manipulation of verbal symbols.

A much longer essay follows, entitled 'Schools are bad places for kids'. Holt begins by noting that there is a desire amongst many people he has talked with, to make schools better places, but they either do not know how to do it, or do not dare. The children are mostly helpless, for they do not know what is being done to them, and even if they work it out, they are told it is being done to them by kindly intentioned people and for their own good. Holt does not dig as deeply as Alice Miller in her book *For Your Own Good* for the roots of this adult behaviour, but just points to its mechanisms.

For the most part, children arrive at school as curious, patient, energetic and skilful learners who have already directed their own learning of their mother tongue and encouraged the adults around them to perform as learning coaches in this endeavour. Gradually, this confidence is broken down by a series of messages, the first of which is that you come to school to learn. But, Holt protests, they were learning before and very effectively too.

The message that is gradually introduced is that children cannot really be trusted to learn and are no good at it, so adults need to control and direct it. The best of early childhood education, of course, does no such thing and encourages the development of the natural learning skills children bring to school with them. But this is only a delaying experience and the other messages are introduced sooner or later.

There are other messages. Personal curiosity is not encouraged. To be wrong, or uncertain, or confused, is a crime. What is required are the skills of 'practical slavery':

> "There is much fine talk in schools about Teaching Democratic Values.
> What the children really learn is Practical Slavery. How to suck up to
> the boss. How to keep out of trouble, and get other people in.
> 'Teacher, Billy is ...' Set into mean-spirited competition against other
> children, he learns that every man is the natural enemy of every other
> man. Life, as the strategists say, is a zero-sum game: what one wins,
> another must lose, for every winner there must be a loser. (Actually,

our educators, above all our so-called and self-styled prestige universities, have turned education into a game where for every winner there are twenty losers.)" (p. 25)

School becomes a long lesson in 'How To Turn Yourself Off' - for, 'Sit still! Be quiet!' are the great watchwords of the enterprise, a behaviour requirement guaranteed to induce high levels of passivity and then stupidity:

> *"... the teachers are no more free to respond openly and honestly to the students than the students are free to respond to the teachers or each other, where the air practically vibrates with suspicions and anxiety, the child learns to live in a kind of daze, saving his energies for those small parts of his life that are too trivial for the adults to bother with ..." (p. 31)*

The remedies Holt proposes are radical:
1. Abandon or modify drastically the compulsory attendance laws.
2. Experiment with 'schools without walls' approaches.
3. Involve many more people who are not teachers in learning situations.
4. Encourage students to teach each other.
5. Let children judge their own work.
6. Abolish the fixed, required curriculum.

It comes down, Holt argues, to whether we are on the side of slavery or freedom:

> *"What it all boils down to is, are we trying to raise sheep - timid, docile, easily driven or led - or free men? If what we want are sheep, our schools are perfect as they are. If what we want is free men, we'd better start making some big changes." (p. 36)*

The next essay, *The Fourth R: The Rat Race*, continues to display misgivings about the whole formal educational enterprise. Although schools may claim to be victims of society's expectations, Holt observes that this is only partly true and that schools are also the source of mis-education.

> *"It is only in theory, today, that educational institutions serve the student; in fact, the real job of a student at any ambitious institution is, by his performance, to enhance the reputation of that institution." (p. 37)*

There is far more concern that the student is not doing right by the school than that the school is not doing right by the student. Indeed, in the latter case, the blame is put firmly on the 'bad' student. In the service of the school's reputation, children have not worked such long hours since the early and brutal days of the Industrial Revolution. These pressures have destructive effects for they create:

> "... an exaggerated concern with getting right answers and avoiding mistakes; they drive them into defensive strategies of learning and behaviour that choke off their intellectual powers and make real learning all but impossible." (p. 39)

We do not give students a sense of mission and vocation, of developing as people, as experiencing the idea that 'every person is his or her own masterpiece', but of subjection and slavery instead. Learning becomes debased and corrupted for it is not for the joy and satisfaction of finding out that students study but to get to something else.

Holt speculates what would happen if schools stood up for education:

> "Supposing more and more schools began saying to colleges, 'Our best students are fed up with grinding for grades: they want to learn for the interest and joy of learning. Unless you show them, and us, that you are making grades less important, they are going to look for other colleges to go to, and we are going to help them.' Might this not change the picture? After all, pressure can be exerted both ways." (p. 45)

In *Teachers Talk Too Much*, a familiar theme in Holt's writing is introduced briefly, of how non-stop talking teachers turn children into bad, passive and inefficient learners. A telling image of the sheep dog is employed:

> "So we have these flocks of school children, twenty-five or more of them, that we are trying to lead or drive down a chosen road. They don't all want to go down that road; maybe none of them do; maybe they have other things they would rather do or think about. So we continually have to round them up and move them along, like a sheep dog herding sheep. Only, our voice is the dog." (p. 47)

Next Holt turns his attention in a longer piece to *The Tyranny of Testing*. His proposition is that tests have no place at all in genuine education. At best they do more harm than good, at worst they corrupt the learning process. Tests have uses for vocational qualifications, e.g. for surgeons, first-aiders, professional musicians, for civil engineers, etc. But testing in school is not of this type for it has different purposes. These are firstly, to threaten the inmates into doing the work, and secondly, to be able to hand out the rewards and penalties that all coercive systems need to exercise control over people. Holt goes on to question the belief that school testing is about quality control:

> *"To me, it seems clear that the greater the threat posed by a test, the less it can measure, far less encourage learning. There are many reasons for this. One of the most obvious, and most important, is that whenever a student knows he is being judged by the results of tests, he turns his attention from the material to the tester. What is paramount is not the course or its meaning to the student, but whatever is in the tester's mind. Learning becomes less a search than a battle of wits. The tester, whoever he is, is no longer a guide and helper, but an enemy." (p. 53)*

Holt quotes the famous study by Howard Becker of *Trading for Grades* in a medical school where preparing for examinations replaced learning medicine as the main object in the behaviour of students. In the task of outwitting the tester, any means seem legitimate and cheating can become widespread.

Other objections are given. Tests almost always penalise the slower and more thorough student. They penalise anxious students who worry about tests and almost always under perform because of this. Worst of all, perhaps, tests destroy self-assessment:

> *"Perhaps the greatest of all the wrongs we do to children in school is to deprive them of the chance to judge the worth of their own work and then destroy in them the power to make such judgements, or even the belief that they can." (p. 56)*

He ends the piece with a vision:

> *"What true education requires of us instead is faith and courage - faith that children want to make sense out of life and will work hard at it, courage to let them do it without continually poking, prying, prodding, and meddling. Is this so difficult?" (p. 63)*

The theme of 'Not So Golden Rule Days' is that compulsory school attendance stands in the way of good education. It is time for schools to get out of the jail business and into the education business instead. The two public demands that we lock up children during the daytime to keep them out of the way and then try and educate them, are contradictory and self-cancelling:

> *"The schools can be in the jail business or in the education business, but not in both. To the extent that they are in the one they cannot be in the other." (p. 64)*

The resentment created in some inmates spills over into vandalism and the burning of schools. Teenage youths rarely throw bricks at the windows of hotels, banks or supermarkets or set fire to them, Holt declares.

Teachers also suffer from the school attendance laws because they are diverted from educational matters into being school prison guards and school police. The primary function of teaching becomes corrupted. Coaching learners gives way to the requirement to coerce:

> *"The results are plain. People who go into teaching full of hope and good intentions gradually become used to thinking of themselves as policemen and of the children as their natural enemies ... It is no more possible to have open, friendly, and mutually helpful relationships between most teachers and students than it is between prison guards and prison convicts - and for exactly the same reasons." (p. 66)*

People find it hard to believe that order will be maintained without compulsion, yet Holt observes that in the Boston Public Library, he saw a great many students of all backgrounds behaving just as reasonably, sensibly, and considerately as everybody else. A key difference was that they were there by choice and could leave whenever they wanted.

People protest that schools are compulsory to protect civil rights, to serve an 'entitlement' to education. In the past this had some credibility in preventing children being used as cheap labour. But times change and the market for child labour is hardly an issue, and, in any case, if protection is needed it can be covered by child abuse laws. But, Holt states, compulsory schooling is now a form of child abuse and children need protection from it:

"The fact is that the only exploiters and destroyers of children today are the schools themselves." (p. 68)

In *Making Children Hate Reading* John Holt addresses a regular theme in his writing - the teaching of reading which he sees as full of harmful myths. One is using dictionaries. Few adults learn new words this way but check out the meaning from context. Dictionaries have only limited use in everyday living and they are made to be vital when they are not. Another is the idea that you must understand everything you read. Few adults do, but select such meanings as they need and skip the rest. The way most people read magazines or newspapers gives plenty of examples of this. The result of the application of these and other myths is that learning to read is turned into a counter-productive activity;

> *"... for most children school is a place of danger, and their main business in school is staying out of danger as much as possible. I now began to see also that books are among the most dangerous things in school. From the very beginning of school we make books and reading a constant source of possible failure and public humiliation." (p. 73)*

The consequence is that, before long, children associate books and reading with mistakes, real or feared, and penalties and humiliations. They can easily come to the conclusion that books are best left alone as much as possible.

Holt goes on to describe some of his own experiences of teaching reading. There was the day he told the class that he wanted them to read only for pleasure from now on and that he would not be checking up on their understanding either of the words or the books. The children responded, after a period of disbelief, by turning into avid readers. Using similar devices, he also freed up their writing with the 'Composition Derby' where spelling words correctly was suspended as a requirement but he offered to service their needs by writing any word they wanted on the board. He obtained furious writing activity with themes such as 'The Day The School Burned Down'. The children responded by both writing more than ever before and developing better spelling.

A shorter essay follows on *Order and Disorder*. True learning is not an orderly process to start with, Holt notes, so the idea that learning is a by-product of order is bound to be counter-productive. In *Teaching the Unteachable* the idea is extended to locate the kind of order being imposed and why it is rejected:

"It would be easy to compile a bookful of horror stories about schools and classrooms where neatness, mechanical accuracy, and orthodoxy of opinion - i.e. agreeing with the teacher's spoken or even unspoken notions of what is right and proper for children to believe and say - count for more than honest, independent, original expression." (p. 91)

A longer essay follows entitled *Education for the Future* and it begins in what is, for John Holt, an unusually pessimistic note. He sets out to write about what ought to happen, but he signals that he does not think it likely to happen. The track record of humans is that of making more difficulties instead of resolving present ones. He is aware of the hazards of predicting the future and of the problem that single predictions lose sight of the fact that everything is interconnected and that a change in one aspect will have a knock-on effect on several others. Thus, the problems of peace, racism, work, leisure, waste, environment, all interact with each other.

"The many problems we seem to face are in fact part of a whole problem. Unfortunately, we cannot say what the whole problem is, except by talking about the parts that make it up." (p. 95)

As regards education, Holt distinguishes between the problems of education itself and the problems of educational institutions. The latter have an agenda of crowded classrooms, teacher shortages, buildings, finance, the impact of technology, and the like. Education is concerned with the fundamental questions such as what is the job of schools and, indeed, do they have a legitimate role at all.

In his remarks about peace, the links with education are drawn out. The root causes of war are the kind of people who will strive to find scapegoats on which to focus the disappointments, envy, anger, fear and hatred they accumulate in their daily lives:

"The fundamental educational problem of our time is to find ways to help children grow into adults who have no wish to do harm. We must recognise that traditional education, far from ever solving this problem, has never tried to solve it. Indeed, its efforts have, if anything, been in exactly the opposite direction. An important aim of traditional education has always been to make children into the kind of adults who were ready to hate and kill whomever their leaders might declare to be their enemies." (p.98)

Part of the reason is that education has usually been nationalistic and therefore sustaining a category of 'them', the outsiders and potential scapegoats:

"When we start talking about Them, those people on the outside, strangers, heathen, unbelievers, then the moral code goes out of the window, and everything is allowed. Lie, steal, cheat, kill, destroy, torture - nothing is too bad; in fact, the worse, the better." (p. 98)

This attitude spills over into the policies towards the poor nations where the problem is not so much that we lack resources but that we are short in sympathy and generosity. John Holt worked for a time in the world peace movement, so he writes here from his previous experience.

Racism is another connected problem where the perceived outsiders are close at hand. It is time to think of the American **Ways** of Life rather than the singular version that dominates current thinking.

The problems of work, leisure, poverty, waste and environment Holt sees as having a common factor in greed. Greed needs to be brought under control rather than glorified. The spirit of one American who responded to the idea that he could expand his business and get rich, by saying he could not eat more than four meals a day, so what was the point, should be emulated instead.

Another linking factor is lack of freedom. Most Americans are not free and have got used to being pushed around from their schooldays onwards. Greed seems like one way of becoming free: the glamorous greedy of public life look free, but it is a false freedom based on the need to laud it over others.

Real freedom has to begin in schools that share power with children and give them freedom to move, plan and use their time, to direct and assess their own learning, and to be treated like sensible human beings:

"If we want a country in which everyone has his place, slave to everyone above him, master to everyone below him; a country in which respect for and obedience to authority is the guiding rule of life; a country, in short, like Germany in the generation before Hitler - if this is what we want, we are on the right track ...

"On the other hand, if we want a country in which people will resist the growing pressures to conformity and servility and will vigorously

defend their own rights and the rights of others, then we had better begin to give children some real freedom in school - freedom to move, to talk, to plan and use their time, to direct and assess their own learning, to act, and be treated, like sensible human beings." (p. 114)

A short review of a book on teaching in urban school is the subject of *Blackboard Bungle*. The model proposed is based on the idea that learning is a by-product of order. This is likened to the story of the countryman's response to how to get to the local post office: *"Well, the fact is you can't get to the post office from here."* The model offered in the book, Holt suggests, deserves the same response, because the model is so fundamentally flawed, that no amount of patching and tinkering with it will make it work. If they started with the idea that order is a by-product of real learning, things might start to change:

"For the slums, we need something better. Any order we get is going to have to be a by-product of real learning, learning that satisfies the curiosity of the children, that helps them to make some sense of their lives and the world they live in, that helps make these lives, if not pleasant, at least bearable." (p. 118)

In *Children in Prison* teachers are the subject of scrutiny. Since new teachers are selected on the basis of their success in a system that stresses competitive examinations and the rote-learning of disconnected facts, they usually carry this method forward into their own teaching. Moreover, teachers are mostly recruited from a similar background. The teachers who appeared in Boston's schools:

"... came from predominately non-intellectual or even anti-intellectual lower middle class backgrounds, and that they looked on education very much as another branch of the civil service ... it was a safe, secure, and respectable way to move a rung or two from the bottom of the socio-economic ladder." (p. 123)

The result can too often be cohorts of dull teachers, prone to over-rate order, anxiously sensitive to their own authority and status, convinced that their message of 'study hard and you can be like me' has widespread appeal to the young. What could an appeal to give children more freedom possibly mean to such people who have never been free themselves? Holt concludes that city schools fail because they are full of such teachers.

In contrast, the next short piece, *Comic Truth on an Urgent Problem*, is a commentary on the work of James Herndon in a ghetto junior high school where his success in making a few things happen in the school was seen as a threat to the system and he was ousted as a result. Dullness won the day.

The final essay is a much longer piece entitled *Talk*. It is an account of a visit to UK round about the year 1969. It begins with some comments of the role of Great Britain in the future. Although economic decline was likely to continue with the loss of all assets of the old empire, he felt that there was a role in world leadership in showing that an industrialised country can be both free and civilised. As events have turned out, British Governments have preferred to shame its people instead with shady arms deals, a fifteen-year long declaration of war on its own poor to enhance its rich people, the adoption of regressive educational policies, and a poor human rights record, having been found wanting in the eyes of the European Court many more times than any other country.

Holt then turns to education and proposes that the 'body of knowledge to be transmitted to the young' approach defies the logic of the times. He quotes the vocational educationalist from the state of California who asked industrialists at a conference to tell him what employees are going to have to know seven years from now. The response was hysterical laughter and the Lockheed Aircraft Corporation representative replied, *"... we can't tell you what our employees need to know seven **months** from now."*

Apart from that, with knowledge increasing in quantity as well as changing in substance, we must all live with knowing only a small fraction of the knowledge at our disposal:

> *"We are all of us, no matter how hard we work, no matter how curious*
> *we are, condemned to grow relatively more ignorant every day we live,*
> *to know less and less of the sum of what is known." (p. 142)*

Since the experts either cannot agree, or need more time to sift the evidence than events will often allow, they cannot relieve us of the responsibility to make decisions on the best knowledge we have to hand. The consequence of this is that we have to learn to live with uncertainty and partial knowledge:

> *"I expect to live my entire life in uncertainty about as ignorant and*
> *uncertain and confused as I am now, and I have learned to live with*

this, not to worry about it. I have learned to swim in uncertainty the way a fish swims in water." (p. 144)

Young children are very good at this and operate with an experimental model of the world. They check, re-check and revise this model day to day and hour to hour. Only later are they introduced to the panicky quest for certainty that dominates the minds of most adults. All the things in school that contribute to this mis-guided quest for certainty at the expense of the confidence of children in their rather pragmatic approach, are dubious. They are educationally counter-productive. Therefore,

> *"I don't believe in the curriculum, I don't believe in grades, I don't believe in teacher-judged learning. I believe in children learning with our assistance and encouragement the things they want to learn, when they want to learn them, how they want to learn them, why they want to learn them. This is what it seems to me education must now be about." (p. 146)*

Such learning can take place anywhere, and it is arrogant nonsense for educators to assume or propose that any day a child does not spend in school is a day lost and wasted.

At this point in the piece, Holt is answering questions put to him by members of the British audience. In answer to the observation that 'in the competition for jobs, employers are asking for tokens that children have learned an agreed, even if mostly useless, body of knowledge, and if we have avoid this we are letting the children down', Holt says that public education means educating the public, and not just the public's children. We have to engage in concerted debate about any false assumptions about education that we encounter.

> *"The case for traditional education seems to me much weaker than it has been, and is getting ever weaker, and the case for an education which will give a child primarily not knowledge and certainty but resourcefulness, flexibility, curiosity, skill in learning, readiness to unlearn - the case ... grows ever stronger." (p. 155)*

The next questioner asks, *"Are there still a few areas of experience through which all children should go?"* Holt says he used to think this but he no longer does. He used to think mathematics was a candidate but is now dubious of the usefulness of it either as a part of a preparation for life or as a tool to help intellectual growth.   Mathematics, he has come to conclude is as much entertainment as music or chess. (In passing, we can find support for Holt's view by noting that the eminent mathematician, Bertrand Russell, came to a similar conclusion.)

Reading, however, is different and is an essential skill, Holt says. But it still does not need to be compulsory and most of the problems children have with reading would go away if we stopped trying to teach it to them in a formal way, but left them to learn it themselves in their own way in exactly the same way that they learned their mother tongue.

Schools based on the compulsion model perform a kind of spiritual lobotomy and are destructive of spirit, character and identity. They say to children:

> *"Your experience, your concern, your hopes, your fears, your desires, your interests, they count for nothing. What counts is what **we** are interested in, what **we** care about, and what **we** have decided you are to learn." (p. 161)*

The final question put to John Holt was about teacher education. In response, he outlined his vision of effective teacher education:

> *"Generally speaking, I think that teachers have got to be given, in their training, the kinds of experiences we want them later to give to their children. I think they have got to be allowed to discover the pleasure and excitement of learning things for their own reasons in their own way. This coming year I am going to be teaching some education courses, one at Harvard in the fall term and a couple at the University of California in the winter term. One of the things I'm going to try to do is to put into practice what I'm talking about. I'm not going to have required assignments, tests, and grades. I'm going to give people a list of resources, and by resources I not only mean books to read but schools to visit and people to talk to and places to investigate. I'm going to say: if you want to know more about any of these things I'll tell you more, and if you want to talk about any of the things you've read or seen or investigated I'll be delighted to join you in these discussions; but **Explore!** There's what's being done, get out and look at it." (p. 163)*

There is a postscript to the book in the form of a letter that restates many of the key points of the whole collection of essays:

i.   Children learn better when they learn what they want to learn, when they want to learn it, and how they want to learn it, learning for their own curiosity and not at somebody else's order.

ii.   We should abolish, or largely abolish, the fixed curriculum.

iii. Testing and grading corrupt and impede the learning process.

iv.   The act of instruction frequently impedes learning, and especially in the case of reading.

v.   We should involve more people who are not teachers in learning settings.

vi.   We should encourage children to use the resources of the world outside the school to further their learning.

vii. Compulsory school attendance no longer serves a useful educational function.

viii. We should remove every possible obstacle between children and any gainful or useful contribution they want to make to society.

What Do I Do Monday?

This book is meant to help people find their own answers to the question, 'What can I do?' by providing a few ideas that will set people exploring. The first half is devoted to establishing Holt's thinking about learning and the second contains practical suggestions based on these ideas.

At several points in the book, Holt signals how his own thinking has changed, and he starts by noting that, like many people, he used to think that learning was collecting facts or ideas. Gradually he came to see learning as quite different, as a kind of growing. To start with, we all know much more than we can explain using language words and many things we cannot even begin to put into words. We have grown into knowledge of what a friend looks like and are rarely fooled by look-a-likes. When we taste it blindfold, we know this is a strawberry and not an apple, but cannot explain this clearly. Holt goes on to give many more examples of this kind of knowledge, the kind we have grown into through experience rather than any teaching. Our mental model is personal and extends back into our own past life. Since no two people have the identical learning biography, we can claim to have grown to be unique. Car driving provides an example of this knowledge and its the models we have grown into by experience:

> "... the driver of a car, wanting to pass, seeing a car coming in the opposite lane, projects into the future in his mind the data he has about his car's motion and the other car's motion toward him. If it 'looks' all right, he passes. If his model is a good one, he gets by with room to spare. If his model is a bad one, he may crash ... " (p. 18)

The general mental model we have developed can be seen as four worlds; the world inside my skin, a second world of my personal experiences and understandings, a third world of things that are possibilities that I know about, and a fourth world of things as yet completely unknown. Learning can be seen as our interaction in these four worlds and there is, therefore, no difference between living and learning whilst learning is seen as growing. Holt follows Dewey in describing this as the 'continuum of experience'.

School can easily become a barrier to this natural learning process and the continuum of experience. When we say to children that they come to school to learn, or to teach them how to learn, we talk nonsense:

"But the children have been learning, all the time, for all of their lives before they met us. What is more, they are very likely to be much better at learning than most of us who plan to teach them how to do it." (p. 23)

The person who is not afraid of the world wants answers and sees life's surprises as sources of useful information. Fearful people see such surprises as attacks. They may feel invaded by new experiences. Young children learn well because they start out with the first outlook rather than the second. But in school 'invasion' can begin, for, Holt argues, one of the things adults do, and above all in schools, is invade, in every possible way, the lives and privacy of their students. They often become converted into fearful learners as a result, and this was the main theme of Holt's first book *How Children Fail.*

"It seems to me a fact that the schooling of most children destroys their curiosity, confidence, trust, and therefore their intelligence." (p. 53)

Holt reported that many parents recognised this and that the common fear of parents as expressed to him was that school would brutalise their children. They would say that their young children were bright, fearless, curious and lively, so they feared what would happen when they went to school. About half the people who said this, he noted, were teachers. Holt confesses he was part of the problem before trying to become part of the solution:

"I myself, for many or most of the years I was a teacher, did almost all of the bad things I have talked about. Indeed, I think I did most harm when my intentions were the best. Later, when I stopped trying to play God in the classroom and became more modest, I became less harmful, perhaps even useful." (p. 53)

Another development in his thinking is reported at this point. Holt declares that he underestimated the damage done by schooling in *How Children Fail.* Schooling frequently damages at a deeper level for it destroys the health of mind and spirit of children as well. Holt is very close to the conclusions of Alice Miller in *For Your Own Good* at this point, for he notes how children are forbidden to think that their human rights are being flouted by the school:

"He is forbidden to think that these people who are doing these things to him are in any way his enemies or that they dislike or fear him. He is told to believe that they care about him, that what they do, they do for his sake, his good. He is made to feel ... he is somehow bad, wicked and really deserves harsher punishment ... " (p. 55)

Holt quotes R. D. Laing and his work on madness where he shows that the schizoid personality does not occur through a falling apart, but a *tearing* apart as people are pulled apart by the activity of the people around them and the contradictory demands they make on them:

> *"Most of our schools convey to children a very powerful message, that they are stupid, worthless, untrustworthy, unfit to make even the smallest decisions about their own lives or learning. The message is all the more powerful and effective because it is not said in words. Indeed ... the school may well be saying all the time how much they like and respect children, how much they value their individual differences, how committed they are to democratic and human values, and so on. If I tell you that you are wise, but treat you like a fool; tell you that you are good, but treat you like a dangerous criminal, you will feel what I feel much more strongly than if I said it directly. Furthermore, if I deny that there is any contradiction between what I say and what I do, and forbid you to talk or even think about such a contradiction, and say further that if you even think there may be such a contradiction it proves you are not worthy of my loving attention, my message about your badness becomes all the stronger and I am probably pushing you well along the road to craziness as well." (p. 56)*

Elsewhere Holt compares the school to the army - it is the army for children. Here he notes a significant difference. The army does not *pretend* to have your welfare at heart. It does not pretend to value its soldiers as unique human beings and seek their growth, but only requires them to obey orders and sees them merely as a means to the end of defeating the enemy and expendable.

Changing things - teachers as 'travel agents'

Although teachers are restricted, they usually have more freedom of action than they think, use or believe. Teachers who do not use the opportunities will find that they are likely to shrink on the principle of, 'if we don't push the walls out, they will push us in'.

Such innovative action as the situation will allow, has to be used to some clear purpose, otherwise it is as foolish as asking the best route out of town without knowing where you wanted to go. Holt gives his destination:

> *"I believe we learn best when we, not others, are deciding what we are going to try to learn, and when, and how, and for what reasons or purposes; when we, not others, are in the end choosing people,*

materials, and experiences from which and with which we will be learning; when we, not others, are judging how easily or quickly or well we are learning, and when we have learned enough; and above all when we feel the wholeness and openness of the world around us, and our own freedom and power and competence in it." (p. 95)

In the suggestions that follow throughout the book, Holt assumed that there is a fixed curriculum and a timetabled situation with which to content. But his aim is to start a process of thinking by giving a few answers, so that people can find more answers.

His first idea is to try and reduce the 'teacher as cop' pattern of behaviour and instead try to become the 'teacher as travel agent' instead. Those in teacher education need to do the same - to give student teachers the kind of choice and control in their learning that they may someday give in turn to their students.

The rest of the book is devoted to the few sample answers to set people working on their own answers. The first examples are in the field of numbers, arithmetic and mathematics, with the intention of exploring the continuum of man's experience with numbers, starting with measuring and comparing. Later he goes on in other chapters to extend this theme into measuring speed, measuring strength and measuring ourselves.

Holt then turns his attention to talking and writing and starts with the problem of bad writing:

"The bad writing from which we suffer is of two kinds. One comes from our promoters, our advertising and public relations men, our official spokesman, our image makers, our propagandists, and worst of all, because more than anyone else they have the duty of being clear and truthful, from most of our politicians, office-holders, public servants (who think they are our masters). The other kind usually comes from our experts, our intellectuals, our academics - and sadly enough, from many of their most angry and radical critics, who too often write exactly like the professors and administrators they oppose." (p. 173)

The first kind is bad because its motive is exploitation or manipulation, the second because language is being used to talk above the heads of most people for display and to try to establish feelings of personal superiority as experts who cannot be questioned. The result is that we feel mystified and manipulated and powerless. These feelings can then fuel the scapegoat tendency:

"All successful tyrants and dictators know that one of the most important tricks of their trade is the art of giving most people somebody they can safely push around. This was the function of the Jews in Nazi Germany. In our society, it is for many people an important function of children." (p. 174)

Good writing makes us feel aware, informed and competent. Civilised writing of this kind starts with civilised talking and listening. Holt's suggestions range from a variety of uses for tape recorders to active lessons using interview techniques. Writing itself, 'making letters', can be demystified by investigating typography. In another chapter, Holt explores the possibilities of using cameras as a stimulus for writing and then devotes several chapters to a wealth of suggestions for developing good writing. (On page 288 he returns to this theme and describes the technique of photoplay using two projectors as a means of investigating themes, and I can testify from my own experience with this method that it is highly successful.)

In one chapter he tells of his own experiments and experiences with marking and correcting work and why he abandoned all the conventional advice on this matter because he found it to be counter-productive. At this point the final section of the book is devoted to more general observations on the state of schooling and education and he first develops a critique of marking and grading. He makes his position quite clear both to readers and to the children in his classes:

"I told the children that I did not believe in grades, that learning could not be measured and labelled with a number or letter or word, that I only gave them grades because if I didn't the school wouldn't let me teach them at all, and the grades had nothing to do with what I thought of them as people." (p.254)

Holt felt this was feeble and perhaps he should have fought the school on the issue even if it meant he was fired for it. Grading, he notes, is often about how quickly somebody learns something. If the aim is for children to learn long division, it is foolish to turn it into a contest to see who can learn it in the least number of tries.

Grading is also an insult to teachers and suggests that no teacher is good enough to teach all the class to succeed:

"They are saying that nobody in the college or department is a good enough teacher to be able to teach his students what he is being paid

to teach them. Nobody is good enough to get all his students to do good work." (p. 256)

His advice to the teaching profession is that whatever concessions we have to make to testing, marking and grading in the short run, in the long run our duty is to oppose them for they are anti-educational. Such a stance would begin to make teachers a real profession. This would not on its own make teaching a profession. This would require a few more radical changes:

"Only when all parents, not just rich ones, have a truly free choice in education, when they can take their children out of a school they don't like and have a choice of many others to send them to, or the possibility of starting their own, or of educating their children outside of school altogether - only then will we teachers begin to stop being what most of us still are, and if we are honest know we are, which is jailers, baby-sitters, cops without uniforms, and begin to be professionals, freely exercising an important, valued, and honoured skill and art." (p. 265)

He is not optimistic that this will happen, not least because any move towards trying to cut down the amount of coercion, threat and punishment in schools, and to work with children on the basis of more freedom, greater respect, and helping them to manage their own learning, usually runs into problems of adjustment in the short term, in an institution that expects instant results. Children, teachers and parents will need time to adjust to a different set of principles and practices, time which is often denied.

Holt moves on to write about children in trouble, ways of understanding their behaviour, and how the creative use of classrooms can be undertaken to enrich the learning environment for their sakes as well as for the sake of everyone else.

In the final chapter, *Some Beginnings* there are suggestions as to how to start on the task of student-managed learning. The idea of giving over a day from time to time for a student-teacher planned day of activities and investigations is reminiscent of the Stantonbury Campus UK 'tenth day initiative' where every tenth school-day was eventually organised in this way. In Sweden a proportion of the curriculum is set aside for this purpose in the legal requirements for schooling. Holt observes that in doing this kind of thinking, planning and working, the students will be getting more true learning and education than under the standard regime of the classroom.

John Holt ends with a few words about how he gave up teaching to organise a group of Associates operating out of his office in Boston and elsewhere to develop ways of changing schools for the better:

"We plan to make ourselves available for short periods of time or long ones - anything from a single meeting or day of meetings to several weeks - to groups of people, whether parents, teachers, schools, school systems, or any combination of these, who want our help in making these educational changes. We will do a variety of things, speak at meetings large or small, show slides or films, visit classes and work with teachers, hold seminars or workshops, demonstrate the use of certain materials, advise on other materials, and in general be useful in whatever way we can." (p. 310)

In response to the people who say that it all right for a famous author like John Holt to talk like this, he replied that he was not known at all when he began to reconstruct his thinking about education - he was a fifth grade teacher who had just been fired from his job and did not know where his next work was coming from. The cause is more important than such reticence:

"Every day's headlines show more clearly that the old ways, the 'tried and true' ways, are simply and spectacularly not working. No point in arguing about who's to blame. The time has come to do something very different. The way to begin is - to begin." (p. 303)

Freedom and Beyond

John Holt begins *Freedom and Beyond* by restating his position on learning and children. Children are by nature smart, energetic, curious, eager to learn, and good at learning and this is clear to anyone who observes infants. Moreover, they do not need to be bribed and bullied to learn. Next, they learn best when they are happy, active, involved, and interested in what they are doing. Finally, they learn least, or not at all, when they are bored, threatened, humiliated, frightened.

Although many people admit these propositions are sound, it does not lead them to reform schools:

> *"What concerns me now is that so many people seem to be saying that our schools must stay the way they are, or at any rate are going to stay the way they are, even if it means that children will learn less in them. Or, to put it a bit differently, our schools are the way they are for many reasons that have nothing whatever to do with children's learning. If so, convincing people that most of our present schools are bad for learning is not going to do much to change them; learning is not principally what they are for." (p. 2)*

At this point Holt shares his disillusion with us. He is forced to conclude that few people actually believe in freedom, although they like it as a slogan. The reason is that few people have experienced freedom and therefore cannot imagine what it is like, and easily confuse it with licence. Therefore, the corporate-military model seems to be the only one people know and understand. Most people, even in democracies, tend to see democracy as a complicated process for choosing bosses to run the country, whom all must then obey, with this very small difference - that every so often we get a chance to pick a new set of bosses. For the most part, people are reconciled to obedience and a modern form of slavery. Indeed the book opens with two quotations that convey Holt's points:

"Fear the man who feels himself a slave. He'll want to make a slave of you."

and,   *"Obedience is the great multiplier of evil."*

The dream that John Holt once had that schools can be places where virtue is preserved and passed on in a world otherwise empty of it, he now sees as a sad and dangerous illusion.

> *"The 'beyond' in the title of this book means, therefore, that we must look beyond the question of reforming schools and at the larger question of schools and schooling itself." (p. 5)*

Freedom in learning is obscured by a false notion of structure. The words 'structured-unstructured' mislead and obscure. Almost everyone who talks or writes about learning situations that are open, free, non-coercive, learner-directed, calls these situations 'unstructured'. People who support open learning use these words in this way as much as people who oppose it. It is a serious error because there are no such things as 'unstructured' situations. They are not possible. Every human situation, however casual and unforced, has a structure. Instead we should speak of different kinds of structure, and see how they differ.

> *"We might say that the structure of the traditional classroom is very simple. There are only two elements in it, only two moving parts, so to speak. One is the teacher and the other is the students. The children may be all different but in such a class their differences do not make any difference. They all have the same things to do, and they are all expected to do them in the same way. Like factory workers on the assembly line, or soldiers in the army, they are interchangeable - and quite often expendable." (p. 11)*

A feature of this kind of structure is that it is inflexible, rigid, and static. It does not change from the first day of school to the last. On the last day as on the first, the teacher is giving out information and orders, and the children are passively receiving and obeying or refusing to obey. Such a structure is also arbitrary and external. It does not grow out of the life and needs of the class, what the children want, what the teacher has to give. It is dropped on them from above.

> *"By contrast, the structure of the open class is complicated. It has as many elements as there are teachers and children in the classroom. No two of these elements are alike, and their differences make all the difference, since no two children will relate to the class and teacher, or make use of them, in quite the same way." (p. 11)*

This kind of structure is flexible and dynamic. It is organic, and it grows out of the needs and achievements of the children and teachers themselves. They create and develop this order. Children are used to figuring out the rules in complicated human situations, Holt observes, but they don't like a structure that is **contradictory**.

Holt is critical of 'progressive' teachers because they present contradictions for children. They speak the language of freedom, but there are hidden controls and hidden agendas:

> "The progressive or so-called free teacher says, 'Behave any way you like'. So the child has to look for clues, which the adults can't help giving, to show whether he is doing the right thing or not. This can be exhausting. Sometimes the kid gets fed up with it, and like the famous (probably made up) child in the progressive school, says, 'Teacher, do we have to do what we want today?', meaning do we have to figure out what you want us to do today? Why don't you just tell us?" (p. 13)

The vocabulary of freedom creates considerable confusion. One problem arises from the word 'permissive'. This is used as if it is a substitute word for freedom. One result is that when we urge freedom for children or for learners, we find ourselves arguing about whether children should be allowed to do *anything* - torture animals or set buildings on fire. If we say 'No!' we are then told that we don't really believe in freedom after all. Or people say, the idea of freedom for children is nonsense, children need limits. All such talk illustrates a great confusion about freedom. It implies that freedom means the absence of any limits or constraints. Holt declares that this is nonsense:

> "As there is no life without structure, so there is no life without constraints." (p. 17)

But there are two kinds of restraint and their consequences are quite different. We can limit choice by insisting that 'You Must Do This'. Or we can say that 'You Must Not Do This'. They are not the same, and are not equally restricting. Telling people what they *may not* do, providing you are clear and specific, allows them much more freedom of choice and action than telling them what they *must* do:

> "A free community differs from an unfree one, first, in that its rules are mostly of the Don't Do This rather than the Do This kind, and secondly, that it is clear and specific what you must not do ... What I mean by

freedom for children - and for all people - is More Choice, Less Fear."
(p. 19-20)

The freedom to have imaginative play is one that Holt defends at this point. He argues that it is in their play children are very often doing things very much like adults at their work. Like the economist, the traffic engineer, the social planner, or the computer expert, children at play often make models of life or certain parts of life, models they hope are a fair, if simpler, representation of the world, so that by working these models they may attain some idea of how the world works or might work:

> *" More important, what makes our truly inventive and creative thinkers, whether political, artistic, or scientific, what sets them apart from the great run of us, is, above all, that they can still play with their minds. They have not forgotten how to do it, nor grown ashamed, nor afraid of it ... Now we know from experience that out of such play may come, and often do come, ideas that may change the whole shape of human life and thought." (p. 26)*

We need **more** imaginative play, not less, Holt concludes, because a society like ours, facing life-or-death crises and predicaments about which nobody knows what to do and about which most people think nothing at all can be done, needs for its very survival a whole new generation of people who can play with ideas, who can make imaginative leaps.

Freedom brings with it various tensions which many people might call problems. But Holt means something quite different. Tensions cannot be made to go away because they are built into the nature of things. There are often two conflicting pulls which are both legitimate. They keep on pulling, and so the tension is permanent. When we attempt to put more freedom, autonomy, choice, into children's lives and learning, whether by making a conventional class more open or starting a new school, some of these tensions will inevitably appear. Holt gives an example of order in classrooms:

> *"Too little, and it is hard to get anything done, or find anything to do. Too much, and we spend more time keeping things orderly than in doing anything with them. Some people are by nature more tolerant of disorder than others." (p. 34)*

Holt deals with various other tensions: Public and common property, decision making, individual versus community, On the tensions of decision making, Holt observes that:

> *"Every time we try to manage the lives of young people, we give up the chance to see how they might have managed their own lives, and to learn what we might have learned from their doing it."* (p. 35)

The tension between the rights and needs of the individual and of the community can be difficult and painful:

> *"When does the right of one person to live his life cut into the rights of others to live theirs? The point is that neither students nor teachers escape this tension by setting up a school, calling it Free, and saying that they don't have any rules. The tension still exists."* (p. 43)

Holt devotes one of the longest chapters in his book to the question of Authority. The question of the right relationships between children and adults is itself full of tensions. Holt proposes a rule of thumb:

> *"... if I had to make a general rule for living and working with children, it might be this: be very wary of saying or doing anything to a child that you would not do to another adult, whose good opinion and affection you valued."* (p. 51)

On this basis, we ought not to correct the speech of children. This is partly because the children are young, sensitive, easily embarrassed and shamed, and might by too much correction be discouraged from further talking. But there is a much more important reason for not correcting the speech of children. It is the grossest kind of discourtesy, unless asked, to correct the speech of *anyone*.

Holt observed that children are less interested in power struggles than is commonly asserted, especially if they are treated with fairness and reason:

> *"As a rule we greatly exaggerate children's interest in power struggles with us. We are so concerned about maintaining our power over them that we think they are equally concerned about taking it away from us. They are very much aware that they are powerless, that we have great power over them ... As long as we don't abuse our power intolerably, or weary the children with our constant struggles to assert it, most of them, most of the time, are willing, perhaps even too willing, to accept it."* (p. 54)

Our natural authority as adults comes from the fact that we have been in the world longer and seen more of it, and have more words, more skill, more knowledge, and more experience. To the extent that our authority is natural, true, and authentic, we cannot abdicate it.

This natural authority can quickly become debased. The more we intervene in children's lives, however intelligently, kindly, or imaginatively, the less time we leave them to find and develop their own competencies and capabilities.

> *"Many of us may coerce without meaning to. The question is, what kind*
> *of influence do we exercise over other people, what kind of open or*
> *hidden pressure do we put on them, what chance do we give them to say*
> *No, what do they risk if they do say it?" (p. 70)*

Holt concludes that people in general and children in particular have much greater learning powers than we suspect, and also greater self-curing powers, provided they are given appropriate conditions. Our task is to learn more about these powers, and how we may create conditions in which they may have a chance to work. Choices have to be real:

> *"At one point one asked the other, 'Do you believe in God?' After*
> *thinking a bit, she said, 'Yes, I suppose so', and then, after a pause,*
> *'After all, what choice do we have?' They lived in a culture in which no*
> *one would have threatened or punished them for not believing in God.*
> *In that sense they were not coerced. But they were surrounded by*
> *people who believed or **talked as if** they believed in God, and as if it was*
> *important that the children too should believe, and who would have been*
> *most hurt and disappointed if they did not. In effect, they had no choice.*
> *There is no use in our offering a choice to someone unless we can make*
> *him feel that it is a real choice, that he has an equal right to choose*
> *either way, that he can do so without having to worry about*
> *disappointing us or losing our friendship." (p. 70)*

In the chapter, *The Problem of Choice*, John Holt opens by reporting the problem that teachers can encounter when they do offer choices to students. They do not always set about choosing anything or doing anything. Holt is not surprised:

> *"First, we should try to see this situation through the eyes of the student.*
> *For years he has been playing a school game which looks to him about*
> *like this. The teacher holds up a hoop and says 'Jump!' He jumps, and*

if he makes it, he gets a doggy biscuit. The teacher raised the hoop a little higher and again says 'Jump!' Another jump, another biscuit.

"The rules of the game are simple and clear - hoop, jump, biscuit. Now along comes a teacher who says, 'We aren't going to play that game anymore, you're going to decide for yourselves what you're going to do.' What is the student going to think about this? Almost certainly, he is going to think, 'They're hiding the hoop! It was bad enough having to jump through it before, but now I have to find it'. " (p. 77)

The offer of freedom, choice, or self-direction to students who have spent much time in traditional schools is not instantly taken up. They do not trust the offer or believe us. Given their experience, Holt explains, they are quite right not to. Students in a traditional school learn before long in a hundred different ways that the school is not on their side; that it is working, not for them, but for the community and the state; that it is not interested in them except as they serve its purposes; and that among all the reasons for which the adults in the school do things, the learners' happiness, health, and growth are by far the least important. The offer itself may be a sleight of hand trick;

"Many parents, and more than a few educators, have seized on the idea of the open classroom, freedom, and choice, not as a way of having students direct their own learning, explore the world in the way that seems best to them, but only as a way of getting them to do conventional schoolwork more willingly and hence more rapidly than before." (p. 79)

Lack of trust in us is not the only reason why students may be slow to use the freedom and choice we offer them. If the students decide that our offer is genuine, there is another problem. They may not trust themselves enough to be willing to choose. We should not be surprised at this because they have been taught in school, in the unwritten curriculum as well as the official one, to distrust themselves. This is one of the few things that schools teach well.

"To choose is to risk. We must realise that when we ask or invite them to make choices we are asking them to take a risk much larger than the risks we have spent years teaching them never to take. No wonder many of them hang back." (p. 82)

Holt reports on the experience he anticipated in a previous book, *What Do I Do Monday?* where he taught at the Harvard Graduate School of Education a one-semester course called Student-Directed Learning. At the first meeting he talked about how he saw the course and what he planned to do in it. He had a certain amount of resources and experiences, all having to do with student-directed or open learning, that he was going to put before them.

> *" ... the class seemed to think my offer and plan were reasonable. Then at one class meeting there was an explosion. They said, 'You don't care about us, **otherwise you'd tell us what to do**'. I said I did care about them, that was why I didn't want to tell them what to do. If it was true, and it seemed to be, that many of them had never had the chance to decide for themselves whether to read a book or not, write a paper or not, go to a meeting or not, then I thought it was time they decided."* (p. 84)

It follows that it is dubious to talk of 'giving freedom' to people. The most we can do is lay on certain choices, and remove some coercions and constraints. Whether doing this creates for other people something they recognise as a release, liberation, opportunity, freedom, or whether it just puts them in a more painful spot than ever, is very much up to them and how they have come to see things. It may help to start gradually:

> *"When we first try to open up our classrooms it may make the change easier for everyone if instead of offering a wide choice from the start, we widen the range of choice very gradually."* (p. 87)

Giving students choices may generate opposition from other quarters such as parents or other colleagues. They may take a up a strong negative attitude:

> *"Don't give these kids (my kids) ideas; they'll just get them in trouble. Teach them to keep their mouths shut, their noses clean, and to do what they're told. That way they'll get along fine."* (p. 98)

In this situation, it may be better to retreat and look for another school. Some radical student teachers are unrealistic in thinking that their duty is to find an authoritarian and rigid school and, by teaching in it and struggling with it, to try to make it more humane. Holt suggests that the task may well be impossible, and that they will just get themselves into trouble and probably fired.

Sooner or later, the idea of freedom raises the question of discipline:

*"When people talk about their child 'learning discipline', what is it that
they really want him to learn? Probably, most or all of the following:*

*1.   Do what you're told without questioning or resisting, whenever I or
any other authority tell you to do something.*
*2.   Go on doing what you're told for as long as you're told.   Never
mind how dull, disagreeable, or pointless the task may seem.   It's not for
you to decide.*
3.   Do whatever we want you to do, willingly.   *Do it without even
having to be told.   Do what you're* expected *to do.*
*4.   If you don't do these things you will be punished and you will
deserve to be.*
*5.   Accept your life without complaining even if you get very little of
any of what you think you want, even if your life has not much joy,
meaning, or satisfaction.   That's what life is.*
*6.   Take your medicine, your punishment, whatever the people above
you do to you, without complaining or resisting.*
7.   Living this way is good for your soul and character."   (p. 100)

The rich and powerful, Holt observes, always like to tell the poor and lowly
about the virtues of duty, obedience, and hard work since it serves their
interests. They want more coercion, more threats, more punishment, more fear
- above all, more fear.

Holt distinguishes three kinds of discipline. The first perhaps the most
important is what we might call the Discipline of Nature or of Reality: if you
hit the wrong key, you hear the wrong note. The second is the Discipline of
Culture, of Society, of What People Really Do:

*"The little children that I see at concerts or operas, though they may
fidget a little, or perhaps take a nap now and then, rarely make any
disturbance.   With all those grown-ups sitting there, neither moving or
talking, it is the most natural thing in the world to imitate them."*
(p. 103)

The third discipline is the one most people mean when they speak of discipline
- the Discipline of Superior Force. This one should be used very sparingly for
it is never good for anyone's character:

*"To bow to superior force makes us feel impotent and cowardly for not
having had the strength or courage to resist.   Worse, it makes us*

*resentful and vengeful. We can hardly wait to make someone pay for
our humiliation, yield to us as we were once made to yield. No, if we
cannot always avoid using the Discipline of Superior Force, we should
at least use it as seldom as we can." (p. 104)*

The eighth chapter is entitled *Beyond Schooling.* In it Holt records his answer
to an African visitor who surprised him with this question: *"If I were to take
back to my country a message about education, what do you think it should
be? "* The reply was:

*"My message to your countrymen might be that you don't have to have
school buildings in order to have schools and you don't have to have
schools in order to have education." (p. 116)*

Holt declares that an ideal system would not have schools at all. He imagines
that he is travelling into the future in a time capsule, and that he comes to rest,
five hundred years from now, in an intelligent, humane, and life-enhancing
civilisation.   One of the people who lives there comes to meet him and to
explain the society.   At some point, after he has shown   where people live,
work, play, Holt asks:

"But where are your schools?"
"Schools? What are schools? " he replies.
"Schools are places where people go to learn things."
*"I do not understand," he says, "People learn things everywhere, in all
places."*
*"I know that", I say, "But a school is a special place where there are
special people who teach you things, help you learn things. "*
*"I am sorry, but I still do not understand. Everyone helps other people
learn things. Anyone who knows something or can do something can
help someone else who wants to learn more about it. Why should there
be special people to do this?"*
*"And try as I will, I cannot make clear to him why we think that
education should be, must be, separate from the rest of life". (p. 117)*

Yet, almost all societies and people now *define* education or learning as
schooling, and measure people's intelligence, competence, job-worthiness, and
capacity for further learning in terms of the length in years and the expense of
the schooling they have already received.

Most students in US universities turn out to be the children of university graduates and this has nothing to do with intelligence or ability. School is a very special world, and the school game a very special game, and people who like that world and play that game well will probably have children who do the same, just as the children of musicians are likely to be musicians, or the children of circus people are likely to work in circuses.

There is an opportunity cost:

> *"Another consequence of defining education as schooling is that as we put more and more of our educational resources into schools, we have less and less left over for those institutions that are truly open and educative and in which more and more people might learn for themselves. One example would be the public libraries." (p. 127)*

In the next two chapters, Holt devotes a large section of his book to the themes of *Schooling and Poverty* and *Deschooling and the Poor*. He exposes a series of myths about how schooling serves the poor. The link between school and the economy is weak. The number of jobs that exist, and the goodness or badness of these jobs and the amount of money they pay, are independent of the schools, of the things they teach there, and of the number of people who are learning them. Schools can only react to this situation. The dominant fact is:

> *"The comfortable and pleasant and powerful places in society are* occupied, *and the people who are in those places are not going to move out of them and down in society just so that poor people can move up and in." (p.185)*

Therefore the message of, 'Work hard in school, do better than all these other kids, get that degree, and you'll make it in society!' is true for only a very few. The majority will be kept firmly in their poverty.

> *"Schools and schooling, by their very nature, purposes, structure, and ways of working are, and are meant to be, an obstacle to poor kids, designed and built not to move them up in the world but to keep them at the bottom of it and **to make them think it is their own fault**. The odds against not just all poor kids but any poor kid being helped rather than hurt by school are enormous. For the parents of poor kids to put all their hopes into getting good schooling for their kids seems to me to have about as much chance of paying off as putting all their money into sweepstakes." (p. 186)*

Meanwhile, Holt explains, we are stuck with old bad habits, old ways of thought, and the deadly consequences of what we are doing. Republican Presidents have been known to declare that they were not going to change the American economic system and its fixation with market forces no matter what it might do to our environment.

> *"Not only do we not know how to save Earth, our planet, our home, our spaceship, our mother; we are not really sure we care enough even to want to save it." (p. 159)*

Alternatives are not welcome news. John Holt knew Denmark quite well and visited there from time to time. The Danes maintain a standard of living close to that of the US on only about one-twentieth of the resources consumed per person, by operating a more co-operative rather than an open war competitive system:

> *"But their average standard of living, even measured in strictly economic terms, is close to ours; in less economic terms, it may well be higher. And thirty million or so Americans are poorer than the poorest Dane, and live in a squalor and misery that they would not put up with." (p. 177)*

Holt goes on to say that in the US, much of the GNP serves no need at all, other than the need for job, career, status, wealth, and power of those who provide it. Nobody *wants* to read advertising or to see TV commercials. Few people would have asked to pay, or if asked would have agreed to pay, for the space program, the hydrogen bomb, nuclear submarines, or the Asian War, to name only a few massive wasteful projects. Schooling is just another wasteful and expensive project that favours the rich:

> *"As fast as poor kids learn to run the school obstacle course, already much longer and tougher for them than for kids of the middle class, we find ways to make the course still longer. It is a great way, among other things, of burning off the political energies and anger of the poor. We can keep them busy for years scrambling and competing against each other for a scarce handful of degrees, on the chance that they may then get jobs that in most cases could have been done just as well without the degrees. Nor are poor kids free from discrimination even when they get the degrees. They still need the connections. Where before they had to run one obstacle course, now they have to run two." (p. 206)*

The irony is that the carrot offered is to 'become like us' - the people who are wasteful and greedy - by destroying your identity.

> *"Defenders of schools constantly ask whether I would want to be operated on by a doctor without any training, or willing to cross a bridge built by someone without any training, etc. Of course not ... But it certainly doesn't matter to me whether the person who takes out my appendix, builds the bridge I cross, or whatever, says 'ain't' or not, speaks Standard English, or not (one of the best doctors I know does not), uses four-letter words in his speech, wears funny clothes or haircuts, or shares my tastes in books and music. But these are the things the schools think they have to teach first, and the children who don't learn them, or refuse to learn them, or pretend not to learn them, are never allowed to get far enough up the school ladder to have a chance to learn how to take out appendixes or build bridges. In short, what schools demand of poor kids, as a condition of being given a chance to learn some skills that might get them into the middle class, is that they act as if they were already in it." (p. 196)*

Some justify schools on the grounds that the students are likely to be learning *something*. Even if they are, they will not remember more than a fraction of it, or use or benefit from more than a small part of that. They are only learning this stuff to pass exams. Most of them could not pass the same exam even a year later, to say nothing of ten years later:

> *"They need a much freer, less restricted, less expensive access to what opportunities there are in society. Above all, they need a society in which there are many more opportunities, a society committed to doing away with poverty and to making available and possible an active, interesting, and useful life to all its members. These are above all political needs, ends, goals. None of them are things that schools and schooling can provide." (p. 216)*

In the next section, *Reading Without Schooling*, Holt suggests that learning to read without school might be a more successful venture and he quotes the case of Paulo Freire. In the north-eastern part of Brazil is one of the great poverty areas of the world. Most of the people are tenant farmers or sharecroppers. They own nothing. They must pay even for the water they get from the landlord's well. They live in poverty, in isolated villages. They have none of the books, newspapers, signs, or TV advertising that surround almost all children in modern society. Yet Paulo Freire, and colleagues trained by him, were able to teach large numbers of wholly illiterate adults in these villages to write and read in a few months, and at a cost of $25 per person.

> *"When Freire and his co-workers came into a new village their first step was to try to get the villagers to come together in a meeting, to discuss their lives, interests, needs, problems, and concerns. Many people were afraid (like many people in the United States) that if they spoke out in public they would get in some kind of trouble. Many more felt that since nothing they said could make any difference in their lives, what was the use of saying anything? Why even think? Better live out your short and wretched life in a kind of numbed resignation. Freire describes the culture in which such people live (the culture of poverty is in a sense world-wide) as the Culture of Silence. Words are not used because they would be wasted." (p. 218)*

But as they talked, they gained courage, and began to speak with passion and conviction. Certain words began to appear, key words, that Freire calls 'generative' words - they generate ideas, and they generate syllables out of which other words can be made. Freire would write these words down and show the villagers how to write them. Once they reached this point, the rest followed. They were able to help these villagers become functionally literate in evening classes after a hard day's work, over a period of about eight weeks. All this took place without schools of the current model:

> *"His 'schools' were altogether different from the schools we know and have, and that I and others, in our talk of deschooling, want to get away from. In the first place, they were not compulsory. In the second, they neither required nor gave any credentials. In the third, they did not lock the student into a prescribed sequence of learning determined in advance." (p. 219)*

Reflecting on Freire's success led Holt to the idea of the volunteer reading guide. The guides would wear some kind of identification - an armband, hat, or something similar, so that people wanting information could easily spot them. When guides were wearing the sign anyone who wanted could ask them one of two kinds of question. The person could show a written word and ask, *"What does this say?"* and the guide would give the answer. Or the person could say to the guide, *"How do you write such and such a word?"* and the guide would write it down. That is all a guide would have to do. Reading guides would not have to do their guiding all the time, only as much of the time as they wanted, fitting it in along with the rest of their life. We can, of course, easily exaggerate the role of reading in our culture:

"From the fuss we make about reading, one might think that this was a country of readers, that reading was nearly everyone's favourite or near-favourite pastime. Who are we kidding? A publisher told me not long ago that outside of three hundred or so college bookstores, there are less than one hundred true bookstores in all the United States." (p. 229)

The final chapter is entitled *Schools Against Themselves.* Holt tackles the puzzle of why schools resist change so persistently. After all, people have been working at reforming schools for years. Not many of the ideas of today's school reformers are new. This is not the first time people have talked about the need for a new, more humane vision:

"A large number of our schools are joyless, repressive, mindless. What is puzzling, though, is why they are and why they resist so well efforts to make them something else. Why is it so hard for schools to move forward, and so easy to slip back? Visiting schools systems and talking with school people in many different parts of the country, I often hear about interesting new programs. But just about as often, I hear another story. 'We had a good program going here a few years ago', someone will tell me. 'We were running the schools in a more flexible, interesting, and humane way, using new materials, or breaking free of the old patterns, or getting out of the building. The kids were really excited, really happy, really learning.' But then, apparently, something happened. The parents complained. The money ran out. The superintendent left for another job, or was fired. Or a new school board was elected. Or the teachers didn't like the program and whittled it down. Or this, that, or the other. And now things are getting back to the way they always were." (p. 239)

Clearly, some of the people running schools or teaching in them are people who ought not to be there. They do not like or trust children. They do not like their work with them. They see their main task as getting children ready for a life and work which they themselves find dull, pointless and oppressive. This means that the percentage of really good schools - enlightened, flexible, humane, inspired and inspiring, exciting, life-enhancing remains low - so much lower than the percentage of school people who would like to have them. But the basic reason is compulsion:

"I think the answer is plain enough, and that we would see it if we did not keep turning our heads away from it. Universal compulsory schools are not and never were meant to be humane institutions, and most of their fundamental purposes, tasks, missions, are not humane." (p. 242)

The rhetoric says that there is one prime, legitimate, humane mission or function of the schools - to promote the growth of the children in them. We can call this the educative mission. But the schools have other missions and other functions.

One of these is the custodial function. Schools operate as places where for many hours of the day, many days of the year, children or young people can be shut up to get them out of everyone else's way. Most mothers do not want them hanging around the house, most citizens do not want them out in the streets, and most workers do not want them in the labour force. Therefore we put them in schools. That is an important part of what schools are for. They are a kind of day jail for kids:

"This task or function of schools, the custodial or jail function, the task of keeping young people out of everybody else's way, is quite obviously not a humane function. It is an expression of adults' general dislike and distrust of the young. It is and must be in conflict with the humane function of true education, of encouraging and helping human growth." (p. 244)

The schools have another important function. It is social role selection. We might also call it grading and labelling. If we want to be blunt, Holt says, we might call it meat stamping:

"The channelling function, the task of separating the winners from losers may be a needed and proper function somewhere, but it is improper and inhumane in the schools. The things we do to select a few winners defeat whatever things we do to encourage the growth of all. We cannot do both of these kinds of work at the same time, in the same place. We cannot in any true sense be in the education business and at the same time in the grading and labelling business." (p. 250)

Another important function of the schools is indoctrination. This means getting the children to think whatever the adults, or at least politically powerful adults, think, or want the children to think. Some of this indoctrination is straightforward and direct. One example is 'patriotism':

> *"It is the patriotism of Admiral Decatur, who, they tell us (not quite accurately) first spoke the famous words, 'My country, right or wrong'. It is hardly ever that of Carl Schurz, a German immigrant boy who later became mayor of New York, and who wisely replied 'My country, right or wrong; if right, to be kept right; if wrong, to be put right'."* (p. 251)

Our society also wants to pass on to children certain beliefs about such assorted matters as sex, morality, corporate enterprise and the profit system.

> *"We are trained to sell our learning for grades so that later we will sell our work for money. Worse, we learn to think not only that work is what we do for money, out of fear, envy, or greed, but also that work is what we would never do except for money, that there could be no other reason to work, that anyone who talks about meaningful work must be the wildest kind of romantic dreamer and crackpot. We learn to take it as natural, right, and inevitable that our work should be boring, meaningless, hateful."* (p. 255)

In order to achieve these non-educative functions schools are compelled to mount an unrelenting and merciless attack on the dignity and self-respect of the students:

> *"Schools do not have the power of life and death over children. But they do have the power to cause them mental and physical pain, to threaten, frighten, and humiliate them, and to destroy their future lives. This power has been enough to corrupt deeply many schools and school people, to turn into a cruel and petty tyrant many a teacher who did not start out to be one and may even now not want to be one. If there were no other reasons to rid themselves of this power, this would be enough; only by doing so can the schools save their own souls"* (p. 265)

Escape From Childhood

It was reading Paul Goodman's *Growing Up Absurd* that started John Holt reflecting seriously about whether childhood was such a good idea. In the opening chapter, he defines the problem of being a 'child', as that of being wholly subservient and dependent, of being seen by older people as a mixture of expensive nuisance, slave and super-pet. This role does most young people more harm than good, so Holt proposes radical changes so that, the rights, privileges, duties, responsibilities of adult citizens be made available to any young person, of whatever age, who wants to make use of them. These would include, among others:

"1   The right to equal treatment at the hands of the law - i.e., the right in any situation, to be treated no worse than an adult would be.
2   The right to vote, and take full part in political affairs.
3   The right to be legally responsible for one's life and acts.
4   The right to work, for money.
5   The right to privacy.
6   The right to financial independence and responsibility - i.e., the right to own, buy, and sell property, to borrow money, establish credit, sign contracts etc.
7   The right to direct and manage one's own education.
8   The right to travel, to live away from home, to choose or make one's own home.
9   The right to receive from the state whatever minimum income it may guarantee to adult citizens.
10   The right to make and enter into, on a basis of mutual consent, quasi-familial relationships outside one's immediate family - i.e., the right to seek and choose guardians other than one's own parents and to be legally dependent on them.
11   The right to do, in general, what any adult may legally do." (p. 15)

The list is not in any order of importance because what some young people might find most important others would find less so. The list is not a package deal so a young person does not have to assume all of them, or for that matter any of them, if they do not choose. People should be able to pick and choose.

Such changes could not come about all at once. If they ever take place, it will be as a process, a series of steps taken over a number of years. Holt is aware of course, that these ideas may seem reckless or eccentric. He is unperturbed:

> *"No state of affairs is permanently perfect. Cures for old evils sooner or later create new ones. The most and best we can do is to try to change and cure what we know is wrong right now and deal with new evils as they come up ...*

> *"What I propose could well take place in any reasonably intelligent, honest, kindly, and humane country in which on the whole people do not need and crave power over others, do not worry much about being Number One, do not live under this constant threat of severe poverty, uselessness, and failure, do not exploit and prey upon each other." (p.18 and p.19)*

His second chapter deals with the Institution of Childhood. It has its roots in ageism, in all the attitudes and feelings, and also customs and laws, that put a great gulf or barrier between the young and their elders, and creates two separate worlds, that make it difficult or impossible for young people to make contact with the larger society around them, and, even more, to play any kind of active, responsible, useful part in it. It locks the young into eighteen years of subserviency and dependency, and defines them as a mixture of expensive nuisance, fragile treasure, slave and super-pet.

> *"Most people who believe in the institution of childhood as we know it see it as a kind of walled garden in which children, being small and weak, are protected from the harshness of the world outside until they become strong and clever enough to cope with it. Some children experience childhood in just that way. I do not want to destroy their garden or kick them out of it. If they like it, by all means let them stay in it. But I believe that most young people, and at earlier and earlier ages, begin to experience childhood not as a garden but as a prison. What I want to do is put a gate, or gates, into the wall of the garden, so that those who find it no longer protective or helpful, but instead confining and humiliating, can move out of it and for a while try living in a larger space. If that proves too much for them, they can always come back into the garden." (p. 22)*

Holt is not saying that childhood is bad for all children all the time. But Childhood, as in Happy, Safe, Protected, Innocent Childhood, is just a myth for many children. For many other children, however good it may be, childhood goes on far too long, and there is no gradual, sensible, and painless way to grow out of it or leave it.

Childhood is a modern invention. Holt points out that children's toys did not appear until 1600 and even then were not used beyond the age of three or four. In the late seventeenth century there is the introduction of special children's games but childhood did not apply to women for the female child went from swaddling clothes right into adult female dress. She did not go to school, which was the institution that later structured childhood. At the age of nine or ten she acted, literally, like a 'little lady'; her activity did not differ from that of adult women. As soon as she reached puberty, as early as ten or twelve, she was married off to a much older male. Children were in adult life until more recent times partly because there was no way to keep them out. Poor people, of course, had then as now so little space in which to live that children had to see and know about all the realities of life.

> *"We constantly ask ourselves, in anxiety and pain, 'What is best for the children, what is right for the children, what should we do for the children?' The question is an effect as well as a cause of modern childhood. Until the institution was invented, it would hardly have occurred to anybody to ask the question or, if they had, to suppose that what was good for children was any different from what was good for everyone else." (p. 32)*

At its best, the family can be an island of acceptance and love in the midst of a harsh world. But too often within the family people take out on each other all the pain and frustrations of their lives that they don't dare take out on anyone else.

Holt devotes a chapter to the issue of the loss of authority of the older generation. He dismisses the idea that this is related to 'being too soft' and instead follows the Alice Miller thesis:

> *"We know that many of our most unruly young, in or out of schools, the ones who most fiercely and violently defy all authority, who form gangs and commit crimes, are those who in their early years were most strictly and punitively brought up." (p. 44)*

Rapid change has contributed to a loss of confidence for a generation that does not believe it can make a future that it will like or trust, has nothing to pass on to the young.

> *"It might seem a paradox that our society, which perhaps more than any that ever existed is obsessed with the need to control events, nature, people, everything, should feel more than any other that things are out of control. But it is not a paradox; like a drowning man we clutch frantically at any fragments of certainty we can make or reach." (p. 46)*

Not many people believe any more that the place they live in, be it city, town, neighbourhood, or country, will in ten years be a better place. The most they dare hope for is that they will be able to hold off disaster for a while and when disaster comes, will be rich enough to escape to some new unspoiled or less spoiled place and live in it for a while until it too is spoiled.

The gap that has been created between childhood and the rest of life is only one of a number of growing gaps. For all our talk about 'senior citizens', old age is defined for many as a useless time of life. Nobody wants you, nobody is interested in you, you're a bother and a nuisance, you can't do anything, and you don't know anything that is seen as worth knowing. Indeed, we are more and more coming to think of human life as a series of crises - the crisis of puberty, the crisis of adolescence, the crisis of middle age, the crisis of old age. It is almost as if the only age to be is between twenty-one and thirty-five.

Inventing childhood has also made having children a burden:

> *"Modern childhood is an extraordinary emotional and financial burden. And as this burden has become heavier beyond anyone's wildest imagining, parents have been told ever more insistently that they have a* **duty** *to love their children, and the children that they have a duty to love their parents." (p. 55)*

It follows that bringing up children now is for many people an endless worry. There is no legitimate way for parents, staggering under this burden, to admit without shame or guilt that they don't much like these young people who live in their house, worry them half to death, and soak up most of their money, or that they wish they had never decided to have them in the first place, or that they could have had something different. The children on their part are expected to be grateful for what they did not ask for and often do not want.

Holt makes a prophecy derived from this situation, which has certainly come true in UK, and also, I am told, in USA:

> *"A majority want the schools to be even more rigid, threatening, and punitive than they are, and they will probably become so." (p. 58)*

In his chapter *One Use of Childhood*, Holt notes that children meet one need of many adults, the need to have someone to control. Adult parents, however lowly or powerless, have at least someone that they can command, threaten, and punish.

> *"And so the family home, which we often hear described as the place where we are free to be and dare to be nicer and kinder than we can be anywhere else, turns out much of the time to be the place where at least to our children we can be harsher, more cruel, more contemptuous and insulting, than we would be anywhere else." (p. 60)*

Holt moves on to consider how the idea of help gets corrupted and turned into a destructive exploitation, how the human act of helping is turned more and more into a commodity, an industry, and a monopoly. He is troubled by people who want to make a lifework out of being, usually without being asked, the helper and protector of others because, unless they are very careful, they are almost certain to define them as people who cannot get along without this help. It this happens, helpers feed and thrive on helplessness:

> *"The trouble with the helping professions - teaching, psychiatry, psychology, social work - is that they tend to attract people who want to play God. Some of them, perhaps most of them, want to play a kindly and benevolent God; others, and perhaps without knowing it, may want to play a harsh and cruel God." (p. 62)*

Holt insists on the right to make mistakes, for most people in the course of their lives will make plenty of mistakes. He observes that, given real choices and alternatives, most people will manage their lives better than anyone else, however expert. In any case, the only way we can fully protect people against their own mistakes is to make them slaves. They are then defenceless before *our* whims and weaknesses. Most people would prefer to take their chances with the world and they have the right to that choice.

In Chapter Ten, Holt considers the competence of children, what adult anxiety does to children, what all this it tells the young about themselves and about the world around them, and their ability to cope with it. It tells them: (1) the world is a terribly dangerous, treacherous, unpredictable place; (2) you are wholly unable to cope with it and must depend on me to keep you out of all kinds of trouble. Such expectations often become self-fulfilling prophecies:

> *"The words 'expect' and 'expectation' are on the whole badly misunderstood and misused by most people who write about children. Most people use them as synonyms for 'demand' or 'insist' or 'compel'. When they say we should have higher expectations of children, they mean that we would demand that they do certain things and threaten to punish them if they do not. When I speak of expecting a lot of children, I only mean that we should not in our minds put an upper limit on what they may be able to do. I don't mean we should assume that they can, and therefore should, do certain things or be disappointed and worried if they do not - everyone has his own path and timetable into life." (p. 74)*

Apart from children serving the need to have someone to control, they also serve the need for a love object.

> *"We think we have a right, or even a duty, to bestow on them 'love', visible and tangible signs of affection, whenever we want, however we want, and whether they like it or not. In this we exploit them, use them for our purposes. This, more than anything else, is what we use children and childhood for - to provide us with love objects. This is why we adults find children worth owning and the institution of childhood worth preserving, in spite of their great trouble and expense." (p. 80)*

This does not mean that our desire to love children is bad, or all bad. We are right to be interested, charmed, and delighted by many qualities of children - their energy, enthusiasm, health, quickness, boisterousness, curiosity, intelligence, gaiety, spontaneity, vivacity, intensity, passion, expressiveness, hopefulness, trustfulness, playfulness, generosity, magnanimity, and above all their great capacity to wonder and delight. It is right to be touched and saddened by their littleness, weakness, inexperience, ignorance, clumsiness, vulnerability, and lack of all sense of time and proportion. But this gives us no right to indulge these feelings, to wallow in them to make us feel good.

> *"But we should not think of these qualities or virtues as 'childish', the exclusive property of children. They are* human *qualities. We are wise to value them in people of all ages. When we think of these qualities as childish, belonging only to children, we invalidate them." (p. 85)*

Much of what we respond to in children as 'sweet' or 'cute' is not strength but weakness, a quality which gives us power over them or helps us to feel superior. We may think they are sweet partly because they are little. But what is sweet about being little? Midgets are not cute for we recognise that the littleness of a midget is an affliction and a burden.

Holt develops his point by analysing the idea of the 'innocence' of children. This frequently means that they are ignorant and inexperienced. Such ignorance is not to be admired, it is a misfortune. Children acting really competently and intelligently do not usually strike us as cute.

"Children do not like being incompetent any more than they like being ignorant. They want to learn how to do, and do well, the things they see being done by bigger people around them. This is why they soon find school such a disappointment; they so seldom get a chance to learn anything important or do anything real. But many of the defenders of childhood, in or out of school, seem to have this vested interest in the children's incompetence, which they often call 'letting the child be a child'. " (p. 92)

Paradoxically, many parents have a plan for moving their children on from innocence:

"Having turned the child into an ideal abstraction, many parents and teachers tend to look at him much as Rocket Control in Houston looks at a moon shot. They have a trajectory (life) all mapped out for this child, and they are constantly monitoring him to see whether he is on the path or whether he needs a little boost from this rocket (psychologist) here or a sideways push from that rocket (learning specialist) there. Is he on course? Is he on schedule? Is he in the correct attitude?" (p. 94)

In his chapter *Love May Not Cure Everything*, Holt considers that there may be some lost causes and that people who have already developed a destructive outlook may be just too difficult to help. Even schools that reach out to such children can fail:

"It is possible to fail as completely at a free or alternative school like Summerhill or Lewis-Wadhams or First Street School as at the most rigid and conventional school. In a school whose main work is having everyone get good marks in exams, whoever can't do this is a failure. But in a school whose

main work is helping everyone to be happy, to love and be loved, anyone who can't do this is just as much a failure." (p. 105)

The best way to escape childhood is to grow up and while they are growing up, children want to be around the kind of adults who like being grown-up and who think of growing up as an exploration and adventure, not the process of being chased out of some garden of Eden. They do not want to 'experience childhood', which means that adults will decide, without often or ever asking children what they think, that some experiences are good for children while others are not.

Neither do they need 'time to grow'. The child is going to grow whether people 'give' time or not. If we want children to grow not just in age, size, and strength, but in understanding, awareness, kindness, confidence, competence, and joy, then they need not time as such, but access to experiences that will build these other qualities.

Therefore to help children escape childhood, they need more rights.   In granting us rights the law does not say what we must or shall do. It simply says that it will not allow other people to prevent us from doing those things. The right to manage their own learning comes first:

> *"The right of a young person to manage his own learning is a right that could and should be granted, and could be used, more or less independently of others. There is no reason why a child, living in every other way as a dependent of his parents, could not and should not have (like everyone else) the right to decide what he wants to learn, and when and how much of it he wants to learn in school, and in what school, and how much time he wants to spend doing it." (p. 116)*

Nelson Mandela vowed to make the voting age in the new South Africa fourteen years because people as young as this fought and gave their lives for the right to vote in the struggle against apartheid. It is first of all a matter of justice. If I am going to be affected by what you decide, I should have a say in it. Furthermore, to deny the vote to the young is all the more unjust because they are likely to be more deeply affected than anyone else by the decisions the government makes and the things it does. They will have to live longer with the consequences of what we do and any mistakes we make.

But Holt is not over-impressed by the right to vote:

"That every so often the people in power have to make some kind of report to the voters, and get some kind of endorsement for what they have done or want to do, is obviously not much of a check on them. But it is better than no check at all." (p. 118)

Both power and powerlessness corrupt people. Powerlessness gives them the mind and soul of slaves. It makes them indifferent, lazy, cynical, irresponsible, and, above all, stupid.

The idea of giving younger people the vote is not a popular cause:

"When I say that very young people should be allowed to vote, many of them react with fear and anger. At one meeting a man rose, voice shaking, and asked me what made me think - he could hardly get the words out - how could I imagine that a six-year-old child would know enough to know what to do about inflation. I said, 'The President of the United States doesn't know what to do about inflation. Neither do the heads of state of any other countries that I know of'." (p. 126)

The idea that adult voters are well informed is, in any case, nonsense. Surveys show that most US people (in spite of their schooling) do not even *recognise* the Declaration of Independence or the Bill of Rights when they are typed out on ordinary paper and shown to them. When they are asked to sign these statements, the most fundamental documents of our society and supposedly the foundation of our political system, about nine out of ten people refuse, calling them radical, subversive, or communist. Yet no amount of ignorance, or outright delusion is held to be a reason for preventing an adult from voting. There are still people in the country who believe that the earth is flat, or hollow; yet they can vote. Many still believe in a literal interpretation of the Bible, that the world was created in seven days or that Woman was created from Man's rib, and so on; yet they can vote.

"There is simply no way in which we could devise a proper test for voters or insure that it would be used fairly and not to the benefit of whoever happened to control the election machinery. The only answer is to give the vote to everyone who wants it, do all we can to see that they have access to information that will help them vote wisely and hope for the best." (p. 130)

The rest of the book is devoted to looking at the rights that Holt proposes should be given to children, one by one, and for the full arguments the original text needs to be consulted. I give selected quotations below to give the flavour of what Holt is proposing in the appendix to this chapter overleaf.

Appendix to chapter on *Escape from Childhood.*

The Right to Work and Earn Money:

> *"Children, of any age, should have the right to work for money and to own and use, spend or save, the money they earn." (p. 131)*

The Right to Own Property:

> *"Today, as far as I know, a child, what the law calls a minor, has no right to own anything. Nothing he has belongs only and finally to him. It belongs to his parents or guardians and is his only if, and as long as, they choose to let him have it." (p. 145)*

The Right to Travel:

> *"To some it will seem as if giving children the right to travel (and do other things) without their parents' permission would weaken the authority of the parents. We should note once more the distinction between natural authority, which rests on greater skill, knowledge, experience, courage, commitment, or concern, and that authority which rests only on force, the power to threaten, punish, and hurt. Nothing that I propose here can lessen the natural authority of the parent over the child or the old over the young; indeed it will strengthen such natural authority as exists.*
>
> *"Children are not indifferent to this natural authority. They get from it their sense of place in the world, a base from which they can move out in wider and wider circles. Their trust in and need for this authority are very strong, resilient, and persistent." (p. 153)*

The Right to Choose One's Guardian:

> *"Children of upper-middle-class or wealthy parents spend much of their lives, and more and more as they grow older, not with their parents but with people who are, as the law says,* in loco parentis *- in the place of the parent. Rich people do not have to bear much of the pain and strain of living with young people who have become too big to be children but whom society will not allow to become anything else. They buy secondary guardians for their children. Most people cannot afford this. I want these secondary guardians to be much more widely, readily, and cheaply available so that any young person who wanted to could make*

use of them. Even more important, I want the child himself *to have the right to seek them out and choose them. These secondary guardians, chosen by the child, could be of two kinds: (1) individual, an older person or family, or (2) collective, some sort of group or community.*

"Let me try to make more clear this distinction between primary and secondary guardians. The relationship of secondary guardian would be voluntary and provisional, entered into by the mutual agreement of the child and secondary guardians, either of whom would have the right to end the agreement and the relationship." (p. 157)

The Right to a Guaranteed Income:

"For this reason the right of everyone to choose to be independent can hardly be fully meaningful except in a society that gives everyone some guaranteed minimum income ... What I propose is that such an income should be guaranteed, not just to all adults, male or female, single or married, but to all children as well, down to an early age - as early as the child wants to receive it." (p. 168)

The Right to Legal and Financial Responsibility:

"Young people should have two rights they do not now have. The first is the right to the full and equal protection of the law. The second is the right to choose to live as a fully legally and financially responsible citizen." (p. 171)

"It is certainly possible that young people wanting to be citizens might first have to take part in some meetings or discussions or pass a test." (p. 181)

The Right to Control One's Learning:

"Young people should have the right to control and direct their own learning, that is, to decide what they want to learn, and when, where, how, how much, how fast, and with what help they want to learn it. To be still more specific, I want them to have the right to decide if, when, how much, and by whom they want to be **taught** *and the right to decide whether they want to learn in a school and if so which one and for how much of the time.*

"No human right, except the right to life itself, is more fundamental than this. A person's freedom of learning is part of his freedom of thought, even more basic than his freedom of speech. If we take from someone his right to decide what he will be curious about, we destroy his freedom of thought. We say, in effect, you must think not about what interests and concerns you, but what interests and concerns us." (p. 183)

"When we put into our laws the highly authoritarian notion that someone should and could decide what all young people were to learn and, beyond that, could do whatever might seem necessary (which now includes dosing them with drugs) to compel them to learn it, we took a long step down a very steep and dangerous path. The requirement that a child go to school, for about six hours a day, 180 days a year, for about ten years, whether or not he learns anything there, whether or not he already knows it or could learn it faster or better somewhere else, is such a gross violation of civil liberties that few adults would stand for it. But the child who resists is treated as a criminal." (p. 184)

"The right I ask for the young is a right that I want to preserve for the rest of us, the right **to decide what goes into our minds.** *" (p. 184)*

"To say that children should have the right to control and direct their own learning, to go to school or not as they chose, does not mean that the law would forbid the parents to express an opinion or wish or strong desire on the matter. It only means that if their natural authority is not strong enough the parents can't call in the cops to make the child do what they are not able to persuade him to do." (p. 187)

"Schools are worse than most of the people in them and many of these people do many harmful things they would rather not do, and a great many other harmful things that they do not even see as harmful. The whole of the school is much worse than the sum of its parts. There are very few people in the US today (or perhaps anywhere, any time) in any occupation, who could be trusted with the kind of power that schools give most teachers over their students. Schools seem to me amongst the most anti-democratic, most authoritarian, most destructive and most dangerous institutions of modern society. No other institution does more harm or more lasting harm to more people or destroys so much of their curiosity, independence, trust, dignity, and sense of identity and worth. Even quite kindly schools are inhibited and corrupted by the knowledge of children and teachers alike that they are performing *for the*

judgement and approval of others - the children for the teachers, the teachers for the parents, supervisors, school board, or the state."
(p. 188)

"They are at least as bad as the world outside, and the harm they do to the children in their power creates much of the badness of the world outside. The sickness of the modern world is in many ways a school-induced sickness. It is in school that most people learn to expect and accept that some expert can always place them in some sort of rank or hierarchy. It is in school that we meet, become used to, and learn to believe in the totally controlled society." (p. 189)

The Right to Use Drugs:

"Whatever rights the law grants to adults in the matter of drugs should be granted to the young ... On the whole I believe that people ought to be able to use the drugs they want. Those who sell drugs should be made by law to say what is in them and whatever is known about the short and long-term effects of the drug. In short, the present requirement that sellers of tobacco say on each package that smoking may be injurious to your health does not seem nearly strong enough. It ought to say clearly that the chances are better than even that smoking over a number of years will greatly increase one's chances of getting heart attacks, emphysema, and cancer of the mouth, throat or lungs."
(p. 190)

"We were a drug culture long before the young started using drugs of their own and getting known for it. Most adults are regular and even heavy users of a least three psychoactive drugs - coffee, tobacco, and alcohol ... We might even add a fourth chemical to this list - sugar ... most of our population, including children, are badly hooked on it."
(p. 191)

"... many adults take large amounts of other drugs. Millions are chronic users of aspirin, tranquillisers, pep pills, diet pills, sleeping pills."
(p. 192)

The Right To Drive:

"My own belief is that tests for a driver's licence should be made harder, that people should have to take them more often, and that people should much more easily than now, and for a wider range of driving offences,

lose their licences. But anyone, of whatever age, who can show that he has the knowledge and skill to drive a car safely and well ought to be allowed to drive it." (p. 203)

The Law, the Young and Sex:

"If by the age of ten all young people knew how pregnancies occur and how they can be prevented, if birth control materials and advice were widely and cheaply available to any and all who asked for them ... there would be almost no unwanted pregnancies." (p. 207)

"Many of our laws on sexual conduct are a dead letter; they are not enforced and few now intend or expect them to be ... If all the laws about sex now on the books were rigorously and impartially enforced, most of the population would be in jail." (p. 209)

"It seems only right and fair that as long as a young person has chosen to remain a child, dependent on his parents or other guardians, his sex life, at least in their house, should be their business. If they approve of, or at least don't mind, his having sexual relations with others, there is no problem. But if they dislike it or disapprove of it, there is no reason why they should have to allow it to go on under their noses." (p. 210)

Steps to Take:

"One good way to work for a truly different and better world was to act in their daily lives, as far as they could, as if that world existed ... We can begin to treat children, even the youngest ... wherever we may find them, as we would want everyone to treat them in the society we are trying to make. We can begin by trying to be courteous to them."
(p. 211)

"I know very well that modern childhood is hard on adults as well as children, that it is as hard to raise a child as to be a child, and is getting harder all the time. I hope that what I propose may soon make it easier for both of them." (p. 218)

Instead of Education: ways to help people do things better

For the purposes of this book, John Holt chose to define education in the way most people do, as:

> "... something that some people do to others for their own good, moulding and shaping them, and trying to make them learn what they ought to know."

He dismissed this view of education and declared that (a) it was harmful, (b) that it could not be reformed, and (c) could not be carried out wisely or humanely. This was because its purpose was neither wise nor humane. The school built on this set of assumptions suffered from the three Cs of compulsion, coercion and competition, and it encouraged fear, threats, bribes and greed.

Education as imposition versus education as 'doing'

His own preferred view of education was quite different but he decided to leave the word aside altogether and talk instead of the contrasting idea of 'doing'. This word in fact restates his view of education which is that it is something people get for themselves, not something given to them or done to them. Holt saw this as a matter of fundamental human rights:

> "Next to life itself, the most fundamental of all human rights is the right to control our own minds and thoughts. That means, the right to decide for ourselves how we will explore the world around us, think about our own and other people's experiences, and find the meaning of our lives. Whoever takes that right away from us, by trying to 'educate' us, attacks the very centre of our being and does us a most profound and lasting injury. He tells us, in effect, that we cannot even be trusted to think, that for all our lives we must depend on others to tell us the meaning of our world and our lives, and that any meaning we may make for ourselves, out of our own experience, has no value."
> (p. 8)

Consequently, the authoritarian school was the most dangerous of the social inventions because it sustained a modern version of slavery where most people were shaped to be nothing more than consumers, producers, spectators, and 'fans', driven by greed, envy and fear. Holt admits that he can expect to speak only to the minority of people who recognise that children, like all of us, will:

> *"... live better, learn more, and grow more able to cope with the world if they are not constantly bribed, wheedled, bullied, threatened, humiliated, and hurt; if they are not set endlessly against each other in a race which all but a few must lose; if they are not constantly made to feel incompetent, stupid, untrustworthy, guilty, fearful, and ashamed; if their interests, concerns, and enthusiasms are not ignored or scorned; and if instead they are allowed, encouraged, and (if they wish) helped to work with and help each other, to learn from each other, and to think, talk, write, and read about the things that most excite and interest them." (p. 11)*

Natural learning

Holt's basic proposition is that children do not need to be made to learn about the world because they are born as natural learners, who both want to and know how to make sense of their environment. The most impressive piece of evidence on Holt's side is the fact that children teach themselves their native tongue and even coach their parents in the dovetailing skills needed to support them in this task.

The advice to parents that is derived from this analysis is stark. Do not waste energy trying to reform these schools. If you can find ways to escape schooling, do so. If not, try to find ways outside school to nourish the children's curiosity and confidence in themselves as competent learners. The bigger task in which Holt was engaged himself, was to 'blow the cover' of authoritarian schooling by revealing the assortment of alibis, myths, lies and illusions.

One of these myths is that of the alleged primacy of school learning. Schools trade on the idea that:

> *"... (1) if I want to learn anything important, I have to go to a place called school and get someone called a teacher to teach it to me; (2) the process will be boring and painful;" (p.14)*

There are few experiences from which we learn nothing, so there remains the question of what it is that we really learn from authoritarian schooling. Holt lists anger, resentment, self-contempt and self-hatred for allowing ourselves to be pushed around or used by others, for not having been smart enough or strong enough to resist or refuse. (Alice Miller goes further than Holt and adds that we learn the sub-conscious, festering desire to take revenge on somebody, and this usually turns out to be one's own children who in turn are bullied into doing things 'for their own good' and sent on to authoritarian schooling in their turn.)

Natural learning is based on the idea that doing is learning. Holt explains that we learn to talk by talking and we learn to walk by walking. But our confidence in this simple principle gets eroded by outside interference. Some of this interference is based on some false assumptions about knowledge. What we call 'bodies of knowledge' or 'subjects' are not nouns but **verbs**. They are things people do:

> *"These are simply different ways in which we look at parts of the wholeness of reality and human experience and ask certain kinds of questions about them. History is the* **act** *of asking questions about certain aspects of the past. So are Geology and Palaeontology, but the questions are different. Physics and Chemistry are ways of asking questions about the non-living world about us. And so on. All of these are, of course, collective acts; we do them with other people, and many people have done them over the years. Thus each one of these human activities has its own history, and at least part of Mathematics or Physics or Philosophy is the account of what other mathematicians or physicists or philosophers have done. But our 'knowledge' of these things is a record of what these people* **did***; what questions they asked, how they went about getting their answers, what answers they got, what conclusions they drew from their answers." (p. 20)*

Schools for 'doers'

There are examples of schools that are 'doing' places to be found. Holt gives the examples of typing schools, driving schools, dance schools, ski schools, karate schools, language schools and cooking schools. These schools differ from the compulsory, coercive child schools in various ways. People choose to go there. It is unusual for there to be an entrance test to see if we are smart enough to do the activity. We stay only as long as we find it helpful. Attendance is based on an agreement that if you will do certain things, the school will in turn teach you what you want to do. Often there is a 'no success, no charge' undertaking by the school. e.g. if we do not get you through the driving test after following our course your money will be refunded. In these 'doing' schools the teachers work to a different set of assumptions - for one thing they accept that they are there to make themselves redundant: when the learner has passed the driving test, the teacher is no longer required.

The Beacon Hill Free School in Boston is described by Holt as an example of a school that is for 'doing'. The school has four sessions a year and each session begins with a general meeting. People come to the meeting to either offer a course or activity, or to learn what will be on offer. Anyone can offer a course and no proof of competence is asked for. The power of the teacher to hold the class together is seen as sufficient and the students are seen as capable of judging their own welfare. The offers are made into a catalogue. Places to meet are located in the community and may often be in the homes of the people concerned. There are no charges. The only expense of running the school is the cost of the catalogue. It has no political ideology. It is just a human learning exchange. Other USA cities organise something similar and call it a Learning Exchange. The one in Illinois lists 43 instruments and musical activities for those who want to develop their musical interests. The chief drawback is that success creates the problems of growth so that a full-time secretary may be required and there can be a shortage of spaces to meet. Although these exchanges operate for adults the principles could be applied to children in the form of invitational schools.

The public library is another example of a 'doing' and an 'invitational' school, even though we do not call it a school. It is simply there for anyone to use if they have a need for it. The services available could easily be extended to encourage small presses:

> *"We have learned, or been taught to think, that Freedom of the Press means the right of multimillionaire owners of newspapers or radio or TV stations to print and say whatever they like ... But this isn't what Freedom of the Press was first supposed to mean. It meant freedom to run a press, that is, to print and spread one's own ideas." (p. 42)*

Libraries could also be extended to the loan of musical instruments and provide music practice facilities. There could also be 'tool' libraries for arts and crafts, for household repairs and for car maintenance. But then, the present school facilities could be made available on the same basis if we abandoned the idea of compulsory attendance. We would need a new kind of teacher. As well as the current 'sage on the stage', we would need 'guides on the side'. These would be learning coaches guiding the learning plans of family members in a variety of locations.

Volunteer reading guides

Holt repeats his idea, introduced in *Freedom and Beyond,* of an approach to learning to read using volunteer 'reading guides'. A public library, or a reconstructed invitational school, could be the organisational base for such a scheme:

> *"They would be volunteers. College or high school students or even younger children, if they could read, could be reading guides; or housewives, or older and retired people; or librarians; or parking lot attendants; or anyone else who in his daily life might come into contact with children or other non-readers." (p. 45)*

When any guide was wearing their identifying badge, hat or armband, they could be asked one of two questions. One was 'What does this word say?' the other 'How do you write such and such a word?' For these tasks, no training or testing would be necessary.

Magazines are already a resource for 'doers' and Holt quotes the case of *Mother Earth News* and the development of more green and independent life-styles, but points out that many do-it-yourself magazines for hobbies, car repair and household repair already exist. Co-operatives for house-building, food-buying and other activities were other examples of 'doing' schools. The existing provision of sports facilities for anyone in the community was another resource to encourage a nation of players rather than spectators.

One development Holt admired was the Peckham Experiment in UK where a health and recreational facility organised as a club for families ran in London from 1935 to 1939 when the war dispersed its families and staff. Appendix B of the book is devoted to extensive quotations from this experiment because Holt was so impressed by it:

> *"No institution I know of expresses so well in action what I have come to believe about the needs of children and adults in society." (p. 59)*

Choosing your teacher

The next theme Holt tackles is that of the relationship between 'doers' and teachers. In many of the cases of 'doing' schools for driving, dancing, cooking or skiing, the learners choose the task and then enter into a voluntary agreement with a teacher who usually breaks down the task into stages to help the learner learn the activity. If the desired learning does not result, the learner is free to choose another teacher.

These 'doing' activities tend to be muscular and should not be confused with reading which is not. Holt has already criticised such a breaking down into skills approach in the case of reading, as a serious mistake.

This model of teaching excludes the publishing of results for all to see unless the learner agrees to it, for the relationship is based on choice, on trust and on personally monitored feedback about whether the learning is successful. Teaching in school is not like this:

> " 'A compact of trust'. Yes - but how can there be a compact of trust when the student is not free to choose what he shall learn, or when, or how, or with how much and with what kind of help? How can there be a compact of trust when the student is not free to choose or change his teacher? How can there be a compact of trust when the teacher may be obliged (as I once was), in order to keep his job, to do things he knows will harm the student, destroy his confidence and ability to learn? Or when the teacher is obliged, if the student does something poorly, to tell the whole world, to put it into a record which will follow the student all his life?" (p. 63)

In Holt's preferred model of teaching, the key task is for teachers to help the students become independent and to learn to be their own teachers:

> "The true teacher must always be trying to work himself out of a job."
> (p. 69)

Learner-managed learning and the question of standards

One of Holt's fellow musicians, on hearing that he was teaching himself the cello, asked him about standards. Where did they come from if he did not have a teacher? Holt replies that they came from the top cellists whose playing he heard on recordings, or at concerts. Standards exist in the public domain and are not kept enshrined in compulsory schools. In many cases, feedback on performance and standards can be compared by using video or other types of recordings and this is used widely in the learning of sports.

Dismissing your teacher

Teachers can easily get in the way of learning especially if they fall in love with a particular sequence of tasks and tries to fit all the learners into it. This is a common problem with school subject teachers especially as most school subjects are not sequential at all. In 'doing' schools this is resolved by the student choosing another teacher - a solution rarely on offer in compulsory schooling.

At this point, Holt returns to his experience in the Ny Lilleskole in Copenhagen where the model of teaching has many of the features he admires. Children learn reading rather than the teachers teaching it, by being available to help on request. The teachers operate as the 'reading guides' mentioned earlier. The usual kind of testing has no place in this approach. The only kind of testing is the kind the learner needs to 'locate their place on the map':

> *"Maps put up to help strangers get around in cities have on them an arrow and the words 'You are here'. Without that, the maps are useless. This is the only legitimate use of tests - to find out where a student is, so that the teacher may better order his tasks, or help him explore." (p. 83)*

Other kinds of tests just induce students to start figuring out what the tester wants, not what the learners need. Their purpose is to grade, rank and label learners, not to help them.

Teaching questions not answers

It is relatively easy to teach people to give right answers but much harder to teach how to ask the right questions, questions that are interesting, important, useful, and far-reaching. All existing knowledge began with someone asking questions and the subjects are records of the answers to date. Thus History is not a set of facts but a collection of reports, often about as reliable as the reports in a typical newspaper. Holt links this idea to a proposition for a new kind of teacher, rather like the reading guides described earlier:

> *"No question, no teaching" (p. 87)*

Even then, teachers cannot give knowledge: an answer to a question is an attempt to put part of the teacher's experience into words, so the receiver gets the words but not the experience. To make meaning and form knowledge, the receiver must use their own experience. The teacher can only try to connect their experience with that of the enquirer.

School books are misleading for they usually record the answers but not the process of finding out. A useful type of book, Holt suggests, would show the mistakes researchers made and the experiments that led nowhere. They could also show how the experts disagree. Such books would help readers to learn how to set about asking appropriate questions.

Natural authority versus official authority

Following the idea of Dennison in *Lives of Children*, Holt draws a clear distinction between two versions of authority, as he did in *Freedom and Beyond*. Natural authority is based on wisdom, competence, experience and commitment, whereas official authority is based on coercion and the power to bribe, threaten and punish. The latter undermines and destroys the former. Power removes moral obligations: slaves have no moral duty to obey orders and every moral right to avoid them if they can. Under the official authority regime, the student has unlimited obligations to the school sustained by coercive power.

Under a natural authority approach, no-one could be another person's teacher unless both parties agreed to it freely. In a situation where people had learned to teach themselves, such arrangements would be found but less frequently than under official authority systems. A teacher-student relationship is a superior - inferior situation so it should be clearly understood by both parties the nature of such a contract, its length, purposes and duration. School is set up on the basis of official authority and not natural authority. It is a compulsory treatment place where one group of people called "teachers" does all sorts of things to another called "students" whether they want it or not. The arguments as to why this is supposed to be necessary are dubious. Holt cites the example of officials who pronounce that no-one has the right to be illiterate. Yet any time I choose to visit a foreign country, I claim precisely such a right. Few tourists would pass any basic literacy test in the language of the countries they visit.

Views of human nature

The common view of human nature is pessimistic and is derived from religion. It proposes that people who are free will end up doing wrong. The few people who can be trusted therefore need to take charge and impose a social order and change it as little as possible. This view is called conservative, or reactionary, or fascist, according to the degree of coercion invoked. Holt sees himself as a conservative who does not hold the pessimistic view:

> *"Though I am in many ways conservative, finding it better to conserve than waste or destroy, I do not think that in order to be a true*

conservative one must take the traditional and dark view that humans are naturally bad." (p. 116)

Although humans have done many bad things, he argues, there are also plenty of examples of the good. We focus on the bad partly because it is easier to do, easier to destroy than create, and partly because it makes more of an impression - it is 'news'. What is true, therefore, is that humans are very malleable and can be shaped by culture into people who mostly behave badly, or into people who mostly behave well. The political theory derived from the pessimistic conservative view has a poor track record:

> *" .. the bad is most likely to rise to the top ... Much of what we call History is the success stories of madmen. How many times, on their various roads to glory, power, empire, etc., must these men and their armies of thugs and killers have wiped out societies far more sensible and humane." (p. 118)*

The 'survival of the fittest' theory, dear to those who hold the pessimistic conservative view, is really the 'survival of the morally least fit'. Holt proposes that people do bad things because they have learnt to do so from their society and not because of any notion of Original Sin:

> *"People do many of the bad things, even the worst things, they do because they are taught and made to do them. Perhaps the society they live in tells them, as ours tells us, that since winning is the only thing, it is good to be greedy, selfish, ruthless, hard-nosed, and tough."* *(p. 119)*

There is no way to find out how much good and kindness there is in human nature except to build a society on the assumption that people are, or would like to be good and kind, where being good and kind is not a handicap. Holt returns to the country that records the highest score on the International Index of Social Progress. (Neither USA or UK appear in the top ten of this index. UK did score 13th out of 124 nations in the late 1980s and is reported to have dropped several places since and may now be occupying about 20th place.) The Ny Lilleskole in Copenhagen is a school Holt sees as trying to implement the more positive view of human nature:

> *"In fact it is a 'doing' place. In it about eighty-five children, aged six or seven to about fourteen, come together with a group of six adults, who work with the children to make a community which is lively,*

interesting, pleasant, secure, trusting, co-operative and humane."
(p. 121)

The school is quite different from the usual USA school and different from the so-called 'open' British primary school, which Holt sees as just another, albeit softer, version of an authoritarian adult-directed school:

> *"There are no subjects, no courses, no classes, no pre-planned paths down which the children progress at their own rate, no texts or exams, no marks or grades or report cards, no reports of any kind." (p. 122)*

Holt notes that he had to see a place like this to have any idea of what it is like to trust children to find out about the world and what happens when you do. The reason is that we are so used to the game that adults and children play in the usual place called school that our imagination freezes. Having seen Ny Lilleskole, he reports that he could hardly stand to visit most schools anymore, even schools a few year ago he might have seen as good. Although most Danes do not send their children to such a school, the approach developed there has influenced the other schools in Denmark. Furthermore, this will continue, because the 'Schools of the Future' project of 1990 to 1993 drew many of its recommendations from such examples. Holt devotes several pages to describing the school and there is no substitute for consulting the original text at this point and reading why he was so impressed.

The teachers at the school have natural authority because they are intelligent, informed, interested, and interesting. They know a lot about the world and they think about it. They are not alienated. They do not hate their lives or despise their country or hate the world, although they want to try to improve it. They like being grown-up and have a zest for life.

Holt contrasts this with his experience of USA teachers and with the surveys about teachers in mainstream schools that show that they read very little - about one new book per year - and are not very well informed or curious to find out things:

> *"Like average people in most modern countries, they don't know much and they can't do much - and what they know or can do, they don't talk about or do in school. In short, they are not people that curious, active, and healthy children would choose to spend much time with."*
> *(p. 134)*

The repeated failure of school reform

As the movement to reform USA schools grinds to a halt, John Holt points out that this has happened before. It happened in the 1920s and 1930s. The approaches seen as 'revolutionary' were to be found in the schools of Indiana in 1905. Earlier still, in 1875, Colonel Parker began work in the Quincy, Massachusetts schools, drawing on ideas gained after several years study in Europe:

> *"Parker began his work of educational reconstruction by tearing out the network of partitions and passageways represented by the traditional school subjects. He abolished reading, spelling, arithmetic, geography, etc., as separate school subjects and had them reappear as useful accomplishments and interesting aspects of an experience which was a united, interrelated whole. On the side of discipline, he abolished rules, prizes, demerits, marks, and the entire repressive apparatus which bribed or threatened children into being industrious or orderly. In place of this repressive system of school control, he worked with his teachers to build up a real sense of community in which people learned to conduct themselves as thoughtful, co-operative, public-spirited citizens." (p. 142)*

These reforms never last long. They fall out of fashion, reaction sets in and the schools who have tried to be more humane, one by one, give up. The public heaves a sigh of relief and all the accumulated long-term failings that set the reforms going in the first place, are now blamed on the few reform efforts and the reformers. Evidence is studiously ignored in this process. Thus the study by the Carnegie Foundation in the 1930s which showed that on all counts, open flexible, interest-oriented approaches led to better results than formal instruction and rote-memorisation, was instantly forgotten.

The first myth that Holt points to is that there was very little of the more successful approach actually to be found anywhere. Ten-per-cent or less of the whole child population has ever been involved at any one time. Most of the schools involved were small. The amount of money spent on them was small. The return of the pressure for formal grades was inevitable because even if schools changed, colleges and universities would not and this always effectively sabotaged change. In the high of the so-called happy and permissive years in schools, Charles Silberman and a large team of researchers reported on USA schools, and funded by the Carnegie Trust, gave their findings in a book originally entitled 'Murder in the Classroom', but actually issued under the title of *Crisis in the Classroom* in 1970 after protests:

"It is not possible to spend any prolonged period visiting public school classrooms without being appalled by the mutilation visible everywhere - mutilation of spontaneity, of joy in learning, or pleasure in creating, or sense of self ... Because adults take the schools so much for granted, they fail to appreciate what grim, joyless places most American schools are, how oppressive and petty are the rules by which they are governed, how intellectually sterile and aesthetically barren the atmosphere, what an appalling lack of civility obtains on the part of teachers ..." (p. 146)

A great deal of the so-called reform, Holt observes, never got past the stage of window-dressing, conferences and empty talk.   In Vermont, the State Department put out a document, 'The Vermont Idea in Education', which was a radical declaration about changing schools.   A few years later, a Vermont teacher confided to Holt that nobody in the State took it seriously and only about three schools ever made any serious efforts to implement it.

This is not about personal cruelty by teachers, Holt explains. Compulsory and competitive schools are cruel by their very nature.   Even if physical cruelty reduces, mental cruelty increases as more and more of children's time and attention are taken up by school requirements.   On pages 151 to 154, Holt includes a kindergarten report card made up of sixty-two items.   The children are checked and graded on these items.   After only eight weeks a teacher was confidently informing a father that his child would never be a scholar, on the basis of the check-list results.

The 'back to the basics' movement in USA was based on a myth - that schools in general had ever moved way from them, although their attempts had met with variable success.   A more accurate slogan would have been 'do the basics better'.   The school Holt worked in had never moved away from the formal teaching of the basics using strict, old-fashioned methods in a rich neighbourhood of well-motivated families.   It was observing the poor results of this experience that led Holt to research and then write *How Children Fail* and start his search for something more effective.

One reason few schools had changed is that, from the point of view of most people, **they were not failing in the tasks people required of them.**   Holt quotes one teacher who after thirty years of attending conferences, training sessions and workshops remarked that after each one they just returned to reality and carried on more or less as before:

> *"... which was to try to bribe, scare, and shame children into learning what someone else had decided they ought to know." (p. 160)*

Therefore, schools were actually doing what most people wanted, although this was not actually education, but a series of social tasks for the convenience of adults. They included the following:

1. To shut young people out of adult society

In modern societies, children are a problem. Nobody wants them around. Mothers are usually tired of having them around the house. Shopkeepers do not want them on the streets. Workers do not want them in workplaces. Nobody has any use for them. Schools provide an answer to this problem.

2. To sort children into winners and losers

Most modern societies are organised into winners and losers and the grading, labelling, marking and examining activity of schools does the preliminary work not only by doing the ranking, but by persuading the losers that this is fair. They deserve to be losers since they had their chance. That the rich children were bound to win in a rigged contest, is undeclared.

For all the talk about wanting all children to succeed, most parents want school to get their children ahead of the others and make them winners. If teachers took the rhetoric seriously and organised learning so well that all got top marks, they would soon be accused of soft marking and be subject to investigation for sabotaging the grading system. Schools cannot afford to ape the car driving test philosophy and methodology, where everyone is expected to pass, and almost everyone does.

> *"... they cannot afford to give all good grades, to say that all of their students are winners. They are, after all, selling tickets to jobs and careers. The more good grades they give, the less their tickets are worth. The 'best' colleges and universities are those that can say that their standards are so high that almost no students are good enough to meet them." (p. 165)*

Schools may pretend that they want equal opportunities for rich and poor children alike but the reality is different. The stuff schools teach are closer to the lives of the better -off children. The language used is standard English, i.e.

the way rich people talk. The task for the poor child is many times more difficult:

> *"A really poor child, to become a winner ... must somehow dodge the low tracks, escape or ignore the prejudice and contempt of his teachers, meet the risks of learning without emotional support, face increasing hostility from his loser friends, and find meaning in instructional materials which have little or nothing to do with his life or experience. Above all, in spite of never hearing it outside of school, and barely being allowed to talk in school at all, he must learnt to talk middle-class English." (p. 167)*

As long as we care more about growth of industrial output that we do about the happiness and growth of people, Holt comments, this state of affairs will continue.

There are consolation prizes on offer which less ambitious parents value. If your child is not a winner, than at least there is the possibility of becoming a loser rather than a bad loser. Losers can expect mundane work, part-time work and a low standard of living. Bad losers end up as drunks, drug addicts or in jail.   Teachers are given licence to impose, sooner or later, whatever is necessary to try to prevent this.

At this point, Holt introduces one of the best short analyses of the hidden curriculum to be found. He describes four sets of ideas children learn in schools, the official curriculum and three types of unwritten curriculum. Teachers could work to change all of these if they wanted to, but choose not to because most of them share the attitudes of the society around them:

> *"Liberal and radical critics of the schools have long charged, I think with good reason, that on the whole they teach contempt for non-white people, women, manual workers, and the poor; a narrow and uncritical, and belligerent patriotism; too great respect for wealth and power; and a love of toughness, competition, struggle, and violence." (p. 175)*

Schools, however, can carry multiple and contradictory messages, so that other critics say that schools teach immorality, atheistic science, and socialism or worse.

The fifth set of ideas learned in schools in are outside the power of teachers to change which is the power to make school compulsory, for most children, with the procedures of ranking and labelling. Along with this go the messages of implicit distrust and contempt:

> *"If we didn't make you come here you wouldn't learn anything, you'd just waste your time ... Even if you could be trusted to want to find out about the world, you are too stupid to do it. Not only do we have to decide what you need to learn, but then we have to show you, one tiny step at a time, how to learn it. You could never figure it out for yourself, or even have enough sense to ask good questions about it. The world is too complicated, mysterious, and difficult for you. We can't let you explore it. We must make sense of it for you. You can only learn from us."* (p. 175)

The enduring message is that if you want to learn something of importance it can be done only in a school by a teacher. It is belief in the Divine Right of Experts.

The aim is to learn how to become the same as their parents, who have learned to live mostly by fear and greed. Despite sporadic talk about sharing and co-operation, the serious business is spelled out; it is gaining advantages over other people starting by doing better in the school tests.

> *" They teach that the serious work of making sense of the world cannot be done co-operatively, but must be done in a dog-eat-dog competition. They teach that greed is not a vice to be mastered but a virtue to be encouraged. And, like all situations that make winning all important, they teach cheating."* (p. 179)

For those who ask what evidence is there that people really capitulate to slavishly obeying authority as a result, amongst other influences, of their schooling, John Holt turns to some of the most chilling, unpopular, suppressed and hastily forgotten research. It is the research of Stanley Milgram published in his book *Obedience to Authority: An Experimental View* in 1974. In opposition to the claim that schools are teaching morality, responsibility, and all the social and civic virtues, Holt looks at Milgam's findings. His Chapter 15, *The Obedient Torturers*, is devoted to an account of Milgram's experiments, and it needs to be consulted for those not familiar with the work. In brief, Milgram showed how ordinary US citizens would, under the instructions of authority, give other citizens they had never met, electric shocks past the points of danger. Psychologists estimated that only 1% or less of very mentally sick people would do this. The results were different. Over 60% of men and women in the samples, in various US cities, were willing to go to the end of the scale. Holt concludes that it would not be difficult to recruit guards for Nazi-style concentration camps in USA (or UK for that matter), as Milgram's research shows. People asked to explain their behaviour afterwards gave the standard response of the Nazis that they were only obeying orders. In response to questions about how they would feel if the person they gave shocks to died, Milgram records answers like this: *"So he's dead. I did my job!"* Morality has now been changed from this person's views of right and wrong, to a concern for how well he is living up to the expectations of authority. Holt links this directly with the messages of compulsory schooling:

> *"They teach people to obey authority, i.e. to push the 450-volt button on command. But of course a compulsory and coercive institution could not do anything else, even if it wanted to. School people talk all the time about 'teaching responsibility'. Yet it is absurd to think that an institution that commands and judges every part of a child's life and thought can make him more responsible. It can only make him less so."* (p. 189)

The research of Lawrence Kohlberg is introduced at this stage to show that morality develops only when people have the opportunity to exercise their capacities for moral judgements. But where in school are people ever given such opportunities?

> *"To talk of using the schools to teach morality is a bad joke. We might as well talk of using the Army to teach pacifism. As Edgar Friedenberg has well put it, powerlessness corrupts. The schools, by taking the power to make choices from their students, corrupt them."* (p. 191)

Lest there be any confusion, Holt returns to an earlier point that official authority and natural authority are different. Milgram's research was about the former and not the latter.

Holt concludes that schools based on the current model are, therefore, bad places because they have bad tasks. Many do not see this. There are five groups of people that can be identified. Some believe schools are OK but need to be stricter and more conventional. Others that they are OK but need more resources and better techniques. There are those who think they are OK but need to treat poor and black children better. 'Progressive' reformers think they are OK but need to treat all children in more humane ways.

Holt sees himself as a member of a fifth group, those who see schools as having bad purposes which require radical changes. The objection Holt has to them is not, like the first four groups, technical but **moral**. To reform them we will need to change their purposes:

> "They must not be jails for the young ... they must not be allowed to rank and label their students." (p. 195)

The near monopoly of school over credentials would have to be broken in the process, otherwise making schools invitational would be a futile gesture. Children would still have to go to get the certificates.

When schools become invitational they also become more flexible. Students could choose different learning experiences in different schools. Off-site neighbourhood tutorial groups could be set up as well as local learning exchanges.

Teachers and reform

When John Holt began teaching, he simply wanted some interesting and pleasant work to do. He did not see himself as trying to make a better society or finding truth, or reforming education:

> "I had no quarrel with traditional education. If someone had said to me much of what I have said in this book, my answer would have been, 'Balony!' I agreed without question that students should be made to learn ..." (p. 207)

Most of his ideas about education came out of the concrete realities of solving problems of how he could get this child to learn to read, to spell or to solve this problem. He came to realise that to teach in a school was about as subversive as working for General Motors or the Pentagon. Teachers who see themselves as radical rarely changed anything, he concluded, and they become frustrated by their failures to teach children to think. They are fooling themselves because they are coerced themselves into doing the business of the school. It was like a soldier claiming to be a pacifist crying, "I hate war! All men are brothers! Thou shalt not kill!" as he shoots at the enemy.

He wrote to one young teacher who was asking how he could change the schools:

"You are going to have your hands full, just trying to find or make for yourself a spot in which you can do not too much harm, be reasonably honest with your students, help some of them cope a little better with the problems of school, and get some fun out of your work. To do even that little will not be easy." (p. 209)

A winner-loser society is not going to be changed by the winners and as long as school remain compulsory, coercive and competitive, any changes will be short-lived, or not go very deep, or not spread very far.

Do we have a chance?

The last chapter of this book is given over to what parents can do about schooling. They can, indeed, campaign to do away with them:

"Schools are not a force of nature. People made them, thinking they would be useful; people can do away with them when they are no longer of any use." (p. 213)

When more parents ask questions about why all adults should be taxed to provide a system of schools from which the children of the rich and affluent gain the most, and what **kind** of schools are we running where the poor children always seem to lose, reform can become possible.

In the meantime, Holt can think of only three options open to parents:
1. Help your children cope with school as it is.
2. Help your children to escape.
3. Give them an alternative.

These options can be used together to achieve damage limitation:

"All the children I have known who were coping best with school, doing well at it, and more or less happy in it, led the largest and most interesting and important parts of their lives outside of school. Children who do not like school and are not doing well there, but cannot escape it, need such an out-of-school life even more. And children who escape school must have some alternative, some interesting and pleasant (to them) way of spending the time that other children spend in school." (p. 215)

In addition the hidden curriculum of the school is best exposed by being honest with children about these matters and expressing healthier values in their life and work. The request of schools to back them up and say that 'if pupils get into trouble at school they can expect to get into more trouble at home', should be treated with scepticism. Often the best thing is to do nothing dramatic, but listen to their children sympathetically, because often what a child needs most is what school is denying them - a chance to tell their story to people who will listen and try to understand. This action by parents shows that they take their feelings seriously, and this alone may be enough to help their children make the best of it.

If impelled to write to the school, Holt suggests something short and constructive in these tones:

> *"My child says this happened. I don't know whether it did or not. I hope it did not, but if it did, please don't let it happen again." (p. 217)*

Apart from that, parents can help by showing their children some of the tricks that will help them play the school game better. The children can be helped to realise that the school game is as unreal and abstract as chess, but beating it requires the learning of the tricks. Useless though most of it is, there are the rewards for playing it well, those of the college entrance and the job tickets. Some of Holt's own books are full of such ideas, e.g. *What Do I do Monday?* and *How Children Learn* and *Learning All the Time.* One tip is to buy the books used in school and especially the teacher's manual for use both by the parents and the children.

The option of escape and providing the one alternative of home-based education is, of course the subject of one of Holt's books, *Teach Your Own.* Starting a small school or organising a group of home-educating families in a co-operative learning scheme are other possibilities. Holt speculates that children learning out of school are likely to learn much faster and better than children in school. The evidence of home-based effectiveness research is now available to show that he was right. Holt ends this book in uncompromising fashion:

> *"Meanwhile, education - compulsory schooling, compulsory learning - is a tyranny and a crime against the human mind and spirit. Let all those escape it who can, any way they can." (p. 226)*

Never Too Late

When I met John Holt at the railway station in Birmingham in 1982 he arrived in the company of his cello. This somewhat unexpected piece of luggage signalled the priority he put on his music in the later years of his life. In between his speaking engagements he would return to our house and settle down to play.

Never Too Late is the most autobiographical of Holt's books and although it is mostly the story of his love affair with music, strands of information about other aspects of his life are woven into it. He tells us that he came from an almost non-musical family and therefore did not learn to play an instrument as a child. He has no burning regrets about this, for he notes how plenty of people he met who were compelled to learn an instrument in their youth had their love of music diminished and sometimes extinguished in the process.

He began to play the flute at the age of thirty-four. He switched to the cello at forty and played for two years. Few adults who have never played take up an instrument in middle age and least of all a bowed string instrument, since it is supposed to be the hardest to learn. At the age of fifty, he took up the cello again and also began to write up his experiences in the hope that his story might encourage other people, above all adults who may have been told that they were too old to begin to play a musical instrument. By now he was seeing the task of becoming a skilful musician as the most important remaining task of his life.

The book recording his experiences was also another of his works about education, about teaching and learning:

> *"This is also a book about teaching, above all the teaching of music. Some music teachers have been enormously helpful to me ... But for the most part I am self-taught in music, and this book is also about that self-teaching. Part of the art of learning any difficult act, like music, is knowing both how to teach yourself and how best to use the teaching of others, how to gain from the greater experience and skill of other people without becoming dependent on them." (p.2)*

John finishes this passage with a memorable observation:

> *"What we can best learn from good teachers is* how *to teach ourselves better."*

A few general bits of information about his life appear at this point. His parents were quite well-off so he had an easy and comfortable young life. As an adult he chose to live with very little money so that he could do work he believed in. He managed to maintain his modest life style without many worries about money. The fact that he did not marry was a contributory factor, although he explains that this was not of his choosing. He had sufficient money, therefore, to be able to explore, enjoy and make music. But his joy in music led him to identify a public need to make musical resources available to people with little money.

There were other educational issues in Holt's mind. He questioned the widely held belief that what happens to us in the first few years of life determines what follows. In stark contrast he proposed that it is never too late.

Another mission was to question what he saw as both an erroneous and a dangerous doctrine. It was that the task of becoming musical required forced exposure, coercion and threat:

> *"Most of all, I want to combat the idea that any disciplined activity, above all music, can never grow out of love, joy, and free choice, but must be rooted in forced exposure, coercion, and threat. Most of what I have read about musical education says this in one way or another. The idea is not only mistaken, but dangerous; nothing is more certain to make most people ignore or even hate great music than trying to ram more and more of it down the throats of more and more children in compulsory classes and lessons. The idea is wrong in a larger sense; in the long run, love and joy are more enduring sources of discipline and commitment than any amount of bribe and threat, and it is only what C. Wright Mills called the 'crackpot realism' of our times that keeps us from seeing, or even being willing to see, that this is so." (p. 5)*

Of all John Holt's books, *Never Too Late* is the most difficult to paraphrase and this chapter will be the shortest as a result. There is, in the end, no substitute for reading this particular book because of its detailed anecdotes and accounts of his musical life.

In the third chapter we learn that John Holt went away to school at Exeter, USA and became a fan of the big band sound of Tommy Dorsey in particular. He learned to whistle along with big band records. Later he developed an interest in classical music and also joined the school Glee Club. His musical autobiography develops in chapters headed *Stravinsky and Woody Herman* and *I Meet Beethoven*. In the text we note that he spent time in the navy and then went to work full-time at the New York office of World Federation, an organisation promoting world government.

Then in 1952 he spent some time in England, returning to USA in 1953 to begin teaching in Colorado, where he stayed for four years. His next move was to Boston where he lived out the rest of his life teaching, lecturing and writing. It was during his years in Boston that he took up the cello. But the success of his first book, *How Children Fail,* led to invitations to lecture and he also set to work on his second book. The cello was squeezed out of his life for a time.

From 1966 to 1973 he was constantly on the road lecturing and broadcasting in his work for school reform. In between times he continued his writing. He linked up with Ivan Illich and was influenced by the idea of de-institutionalisation. Institutions had taken over peoples' lives. People had come to believe that anything and everything they wanted or needed could only be supplied by some complicated, large, expensive, and run-from-the-top organisation. Holt favoured de-institutionalisation and set about supporting the idea that people could act directly and co-operatively to satisfy their needs. Learning the cello now seemed an integral part of that concern, so he began again in 1973:

> *"If I could learn to play the cello well, as I thought I could, I could show by my own example that we all have greater powers than we think, that whatever we want to learn or learn to do, we probably can learn, that our lives and possibilities are not determined and fixed by what happened to us when we were little, or what experts say we can and cannot do. In my work with the cello, I might also find out things about learning music that might help many other adults learn it, or whatever else they wanted to learn. ... In short, my love for music now seemed joined to my love of teaching and to my deepest political*

concerns. The gap I had felt between my work and my hobby had disappeared." (p. 185-6)

In his reflections on his own learning of the cello, many of Holt's ideas about effective learning are reinforced. The trouble with most teachers, whether of music or anything else, is that they act on the false assumption that learning is the result of teaching and even, in many cases, that learning **can only** be the result of teaching. Consequently, there is often an angry reaction to the idea that students might find out for themselves and an even angrier reaction to the idea that they would be better off by so doing:

> *"It is not enough for them to be helpful and useful to their students; they need to feel that their students could not get along without them.*

> *"All my own work as a teacher and learner has led me to believe quite the opposite, that teaching is a very strong medicine, which like all strong medicines can quickly and easily turn into a poison. At the right time, (i.e. when the student has asked for it) and in very small doses, it can indeed help learning. But at the wrong times, or in too large doses, it will slow down learning or prevent it altogether." (p.209)*

Fellow students have also absorbed the myth, for when Holt was asked by musicians who he was studying the cello with, and he replied that he was teaching himself for the time being, they were surprised, or indignant, or even angry. It follows that Holt's definition of a good teacher will also surprise, cause indignation or even anger:

> *"... the teacher I need must accept that he or she is my partner and helper and not my boss, that in this journey of musical exploration and adventure, I am the captain. Expert guides and pilots I can use, no doubt about it. But it is my expedition, I gain the most if it succeeds and lose the most if it fails, and I must remain in charge." (p.217)*

At this time, 1973, John Holt was also working on his book *Instead of Education*. But his work on the cello was no longer neglected. He applied the advice of Matthew Arnold to 'clear a space'. In other words, he stopped doing some things that he enjoyed in order to give time to his music. These included sailing, swimming, camping, mountain backpacking, skiing, squash, tennis, soccer. He reports no regrets, for he saw music as athletics, as a sport more difficult and fascinating than any he had ever played. There was enough teamwork and split-second timing in playing in an orchestra as in any sport. It was also a limitless field for thought, invention and experiment.

He also reduced his general reading. The huge stacks of magazines and books he had always read were drastically reduced in number for he already had considerable understanding. In any case he noted that he already had all the bad news he could stand.

His concern for education now took a different form for he changed emphasis from giving his time to trying to improve schools to supporting home-based education.:

> *"For many years, with many others, I tried to make schools more kindly, interesting, competent, and serious. It now seems clear that in the near future this will not happen, mostly because there are so few people, in or out of schools, who want it to happen. To those few people who can't stand what schools are doing to their children, I now urge that they look for ways to take their children out altogether and have them learn at home. To help them do this I have begun to publish a newsletter,* Growing Without Schooling.*" (p. 240)*

But his work and development as a musician continued up until his death. He was conscious that he had not encountered any limitations because of his late start in music. He remained convinced from his own experience that 'it was never too late':

> *"If Nature has waiting for me up the road some kind of impassable barrier, she has so far given me no clear signs of it." (p.242)*

Teach Your Own

Teach Your Own was published in 1981. In it John Holt set himself three tasks. Firstly, he wanted to set out the case for home-based education. Next he set out to report on the wealth of experience of those who were taking this path. Finally, he intended the book to be a manual for action and inspiration for those just setting out.

The book marks a significant change in Holt's thinking about education. With the success of his first two books, *How Children Fail* and *How Children Learn*, he had found himself busy as a lecturer in USA and overseas, on the theme of making school into places where children would be independent and self-directing learners. For a while, he and his allies assumed that such changes might well take place in many schools, and in time, in most schools.

By 1968, however, John Holt had begun to confront the issue of compulsion :

> *"But by 1968 or so I had come to feel strongly that the kinds of changes I wanted to see in schools, above all the ways teachers related to students, could not happen as long as schools were compulsory ... Since compulsory school attendance laws force teachers to do police work and so prevent them from doing real teaching, it would be in their best interests, as well as those of parents and children, to have these laws repealed, or at least greatly modified." (p2)*

Yet, even as he and others lobbied for reforms along these lines in the USA the situation began to change. For a while, he noted, school reform was in fashion, but then it went out of fashion. Holt confesses that he had not learned that in today's mass media world, ideas go in and out of fashion as quickly as clothes.

Facing up to the regressives in the USA

Regressive America began to re-assert itself. Indeed, he concluded that regressive attitudes might even make up the majority view.

> *"Very few people, inside the schools or out, were willing to support or even tolerate giving more freedom, choice and self-direction to children." (p.4)*

He saw that freedom had not been treated as a serious proposition but as a trick, a motivational device. When the trick did not bring quick results it was soon abandoned. This led him to write the two books, *Escape From Childhood* and *Instead of Education,* where he explored the uncomfortable idea that most adults in the USA actively distrust and rather dislike most children, sometimes even their own. He proposed that people whose lives are hard or boring or painful or meaningless - people who suffer - tend to resent those who seem to suffer less than they do, and will make them suffer if they can. People in chains with no apparent hope of losing them, want to put chains on others.

> *"In short, it was becoming clear to me that the great majority of boring, regimented schools were doing exactly what most people wanted them to do. Teach children about Reality. Teach them that Life Is No Picnic. Teach them to Shut Up And Do What You're Told." (p.4)*

John Holt was not impressed by such schools. He said of them that they demonstrated that a school based on such a view was not just a good idea gone wrong, but a bad idea from the start. He concluded that 'Back To The Basics' was really code for 'No More Fun And Games In School'. Most adults in the USA, he observed, do not care all that much about reading as such, since they read little themselves. Like most Americans, young or old, they spend much of their leisure time watching T.V.

> *"What they want their children to learn is how to work. By that they don't mean to do good and skilful work they can be proud of. They don't have that kind of work themselves, and never expect to. They don't even call that 'work'. They want their children, when their time comes, to be able and willing, to hold down full-time painful jobs of their own. The best way to get them ready to do this is to make school as much like a full-time painful job as possible." (p. 5)*

This was not just a working class attitude, he noted. A middle class couple who had transferred their son to the school Holt was teaching in were pleased that there had been a great improvement in both their son's studies and his behaviour, but expressed their anxieties thus:

> *"You know, his father and I worry a little about how much fun he is having in school. After all, he is going to have to spend the*

rest of his life doing things he doesn't like, and he may as well get used to it now." (p. 8)

The reasons for these bleak attitudes were not cruelty or mean-spiritedness, but **fatalism**. In their view, this was how the world was and that it was not going to change for the better. In addition such people had developed faith in violence as a way to solve problems despite the evidence of its failure. Whilst such parents were in a majority, John Holt concluded, any general movement for school reform was doomed.

There had been early signs. In one large meeting the friendly reception for Holt's ideas was suddenly shattered by someone asking in a harsh and angry voice, *"What do you do with the children who are just plain lazy?"* The entire audience burst into loud applause. The silent majority had spoken and expressed its view that children were just no good, not to be trusted and needed compulsion.

The effect of compulsory schooling on teachers Holt saw as demeaning. Since compulsory school attendance laws force teachers to do police work anyway, real teaching becomes more and more difficult. If you add to this the requirement to implement a regressive vision of education of the 'No More Fun in Schools' variety, teaching increasingly becomes a grim and repressive task. It would be to the teachers' best interests to do away with compulsion. and establish instead what I have called elsewhere the 'Invitational School'.

As regressive ideas came back into fashion, John Holt decided to work with the minority of more optimistic parents who wanted something different and who were active in setting up small alternative schools. These usually struggled because of the problems of finance. But some of these parents had begun to educate their children at home and needed support. Therefore, John Holt established a service organisation called, *Growing Without Schooling*. Home-based education became the focus of his writing and activity. His work, and the work of many others, has borne fruit. Today, over one million families in the USA are engaged in home-based education. Home-based education in USA has its own research journal, its own publishing house, and an impressive range of commercial publications and services.

The motives for home-based education

Three main reasons are given for why people take their children out of school to educate them at home. One is that the families decide that raising children is their business and not that of the government. A second is that the parents enjoy being with their children whilst watching and helping them learn: they do not want to give this up to complete strangers called teachers. Thirdly, they want to prevent their children from being unnecessarily hurt, whether mentally, spiritually or physically. All kinds of people can and do home-educate for one or more of the above reasons. The number involved, however, remains a matter of intelligent guesswork rather than complete accuracy. In 1994 it was estimated that over one million families were involved and a figure of one and a half million has been suggested.

I have found people are quick to construct stereotypes of families opting for home-based education from guesswork and they usually start by assuming that the people concerned are rich people. Holt confirms my own experience that this is false:

> *"We have almost no correspondence with people who, judging by their addresses, writing paper, businesses etc., were obviously rich. Most families who write to us have incomes well below the national average ... " (p. 14)*

He goes on to say that they are quite average in everything except stubbornness, courage, independence, and trust in themselves and their children. They have also learned to be critical of what schools actually achieve in general, and for their children in particular.

Some, like Holt himself, go on to question the notion of compulsory schooling as a serious infringement of civil liberties, even if the schools were to become more humane and effective. Holt develops a list of ten ways in which the civil liberties of children are violated including secret record-keeping and testing by compulsion (see p.20).

On the theme of protecting children from harm, the experience of families who see alert, lively-minded children become subdued and lose their sparkle and their smiles after starting school, is a common reason for beginning to review the wisdom of agreeing to send them in the first place. Taking the children out of school is seen as preventing any further damage before a kind of healing takes place.

"... It was the disappearance of a smile, a simple thing, that led Ms. O'Shea, a certified elementary school teacher, to question the value of public education.

"'When Kim was little, she was such a happy, laughy little person. When she went to school, that completely changed. She stopped smiling. She went for six months, and she was very unhappy. It was weird. When I went to the school, the teacher kept apologising for the noise, and I thought, There's not any noise. These kids are like little robots.'" (p.33)

Common objections to home-based education

The case for home-based education is next tackled by John Holt by dealing with the common questions he encountered in discussions and correspondence. The first of these is the 'social glue' question of whether the compulsory school is required to give a sense of unity to a fragmented population. Some kinds of community gathering and activity might help here, Holt says, but not the kind of schools we have now which are set up to divide people into winners and losers and preparing young people for a lifetime of winning or losing. The losers are then fated to look for others to look down on to make themselves feel a bit better. Home-based education is more hopeful:

"Most children who learn without school, or who go only when they want to, grow up with a much stronger sense of their own dignity and worth, and therefore, with much less need to despise and hate others." (p. 37)

Such people can *afford* to be kind, patient, generous, forgiving, tolerant as a kind of surplus, or an overflowing from people who are secure in having love and respect for themselves, and therefore have energy and concern that they can devote to others.

A second question is that of the social mixing school are said to provide. In reality, Holt observes, no such thing happens. Children spend most of their school hours in the same group of the same age and since most schools eventually stream children for examination purposes, the experience of different people narrows as they get older. The result of this is commonly called 'the tyranny of the peer group' and the power of the youth culture that is formed in the process is a widely recognised phenomenon. It is no surprise, therefore, that the research shows home-educated children are more emotionally secure, more independent, more socially skilled and more socially experienced. Whilst the schooled are locked in to the company of each other for 15,000 hours, the home-educated are often out and about in society mixing with all kinds of people.

A third and much more difficult question is that of parents with narrow visions. Holt starts from the proposition that in a free country as opposed to a police state, as long as you obey the law, you can believe what you like. In any case who is to say what is for certain true, and which set of ideas is to be imposed? Schools act as if they have decided this issue and yet many people are disgusted with the outcome. Then there is the practical issue of whether schools are actually any good at changing attitudes:

> *"Even if we could agree that the school should try to stamp out narrow and bigoted ideas, we would still have to ask ourselves, does this work? Clearly it doesn't ... If the schools were as good as they claim at stamping out prejudice, there ought not to be any left. A quick glance at any day's news will show that there is plenty left." (p.42)*

The next two questions are often asked close together but can be seen to cancel each other out. One is about school teaching children to fit into a mass society. The other is about school preventing children from being solely exposed to the values of a mass society by providing other values. School can either teach the values of the mass society or try to give an antidote. They cannot do both. In fact, Holt continues, schools are usually more concerned to induce conformity with mass society values than provide resistance to it, as shown in the commonly expressed concern that children educated at home might become 'outsiders' or 'fail to adjust' to society.

Holt gives the example of a journalist friend who spend time in schools to find out what young people were mostly interested in, and found that it was money, sex and drugs rather than, say, building a better world. Whatever effort schools have put into resisting the values of the commercial culture seems to have been unsuccessful.

The next question is often the first question people ask when startled by the news that some people prefer home-based education. It is, *"If children are taught at home, won't they miss the valuable social life of the school?"* But it is social life that is often the reason why people pull out of school. Its quality is usually mean-spirited, competitive, exclusive, status-seeking, snobbish, and fad and fashion dominated. Parents watch helplessly as their child who was a person becomes a stranger dominated by peer influence.

> *"I remember my sister saying of one of her children, then five, that she never really did anything mean or silly until she went to school - a nice school, by the way, in a nice small town." (p.45)*

In response to this analysis, Holt reports that not once did he encounter the response that he was completely mistaken and that the social life of school was kindly, generous, supporting, democratic, friendly, loving and good for children. The response was that this was what they would meet in Real Life, so they had better be toughened-up and get used to it. 'Toughening-up' often meant being persuaded to become a cigarette smoker, or regular drinker, or to try drugs.

> *"Of course, children who spend almost all of their time in groups of other people their own age, shut out of society's serious work and concerns, with almost no contact with adults except child-watchers, are going to feel that what 'all the other kids' are doing is the right, the best, the only thing to do." (p.50)*

In dealing with the question of children being taught by the unqualified, John Holt sets out to demystify teaching and learning. The fact is, he explains, there is no agreement amongst educators about what is good teaching and the dismal record of schools is proof of this. Humans have been sharing information and skills with the young for centuries using a few simple common-sense ideas:

> *"For a long, long time, people who were good at sharing what they knew have realised certain things: (1) to help people learn something, you must first understand what they already know; (2) showing people how to do something is better than telling them and letting them do it is best of all; (3) you mustn't tell or show too much at once, since people digest new ideas slowly and must feel secure with new skills or knowledge before they are ready for more; (4) you must give people as much time as they want and need to absorb what you have shown or told them; (5) instead of testing their understanding with questions you must let them show how much or how little they understand by the questions they ask you; (6) you must not get impatient or angry when people do not*

understand; (7) scaring people only blocks learning, and so on."
(p.52)

Parents using these principles can cope as well as any certified teacher and Holt quotes a court case in Kentucky where the verdict was that there was not *"a scintilla of evidence"* that certificated teachers produced better results.   The additional advantages to students learning at home are that their parents are not distracted by the problems of managing a class; they know the children better, including their spoken and unspoken signals, and they care more about them - they are not doing it to earn a salary.   Also, they are not bound by the constipated knowledge formulas of school, for as one home-schooling mother wrote to John Holt after she anxiously aped the school curriculum at home, her children protested that if they were going to have to spend their time 'doing this school junk', they would rather do it at school.

But parents who offer their children the chance to have a home-based education need other 'qualifications' than teacher certification:

> *"We can sum up very quickly what people need to teach their own children.   First of all, they have to like them, enjoy their company, their physical presence, their energy, foolishness, and passion.   They have to enjoy all their talk and questions, and enjoy equally trying to answer those questions.   They have to think of their children as friends, indeed very close friends, have to feel happier when they are near and miss them when they are away.   They have to trust them as people, respect their fragile dignity, treat them with courtesy, take them seriously.   They have to feel in their own hearts some of their children's wonder, curiosity, and excitement about the world.   And they have to have enough confidence in themselves, scepticism about experts, and willingness to be different from most people, to take on themselves the responsibility for their children's learning." (p.57)*

Only a minority of parents start out with all these qualities.   Some of these qualities are gained or strengthened along the way. But most will have exercised many of these qualities in bringing up their young children, so they are not outside their capabilities or experience.

Having dealt with the main questions, a few others that crop up are now dealt with by Holt.   For example,

"How am I going to teach my child six hours a day?"
The answer given, is that what they get at school is closer to fifteen minutes a week of personal attention.
"I don't want to feel I am sheltering my children or running away from adversity."
The answer given, is that is your job as a parent and you would not starve your children just because many children in the world are starved, so if you think school is bad, you should give your children something better.
"I value their learning how to handle challenges and problems."

Holt responds:

> *"To learn to know oneself, and to find a life worth living and work worth doing, is problem and challenge enough, without having to waste time on the fake and unworthy challenges of school - pleasing the teacher, staying out of trouble, fitting in with the gang, being popular, doing what everyone else does." (p.64 -5)*

The politics of home-based education

In this section, some political aspects of home-based education are considered. The first is social change. Important changes only occur when people change their lives not their political parties or political beliefs. Thus grassroots inspired changes like more healthy eating inspired by vegetarians, or non-smoking groups achieving smoking-free public places, or humanists pioneering non-religious funerals, weddings and naming ceremonies for non-believers occur in this way. People do not change their lives because they lose an argument but because they come to decide in favour of action. It was for this reason that John Holt gave up arguing with educationalists in lectures and writing as a waste of time, and decided to seek out those who wanted to change things and work with them. At first this was the small school movement, but they found it hard to survive and difficult to grow. Home-schoolers, however, could survive and grow. With help and support they did. Holt proposes a different idea of leadership from the guru model. In grassroots social change everyone is a leader:

> *"Leaders are not what many people think - people with huge crowds following them. Leaders are people who go their own way without caring, or even looking to see whether* anyone *is following them. "Leadership qualities" are not the qualities that enable people to attract followers, but those that enable them to*

do without them ... This is the opposite of the 'charisma' that we hear so much about. Charismatic leaders make us think, 'Oh, if only I could do that, be like that.' True leaders make us think, 'If they can do that ... I can do it too.' They do not make people into followers, but into new leaders." (p.68)

Consequently, in the movement for home-based education, everyone becomes a general.

The next question dealt with is that of the plea to stay in schools and make them better. Those who plead thus believe that school were invented to give the poor a better chance. This is an illusion, Holt declares. Schools actually favour those already privileged. A few poor children do make it through the system, just enough to keep the myth alive and to fool people into thinking it is a fair race.

"Schools like to say they create and spread knowledge. It would be closer to the truth to say that they collect and hoard knowledge, corner the market on it if they can, so that they can sell it at the highest possible price. That's why they want everyone to believe that only what is learned at school is worth anything. But this idea, as much as any other, freezes the class structure of society and locks the poor into poverty." (p.72)

Some working class families believe they will be targeted by the authorities if they opt for home-based education. Holt responds that in his experience, if the schools are in a hounding mood, they will hound anybody and, indeed, worry more about losing middle class children who might do well in examinations. Nevertheless, bullies take on those they think are the weakest, so 'bullying' schools may see working class families or single parents as their easy target, and this does sometimes happen. His *Growing Without Schooling* group tried to give the necessary support when this happened.

How to opt out of schooling

Parents wanting practical advice on how to get started need to consult this part of Holt's book. It is forty pages full of ideas for preparing the case for schools and education authorities. There are model letters and some of the official replies that resulted. I know from my experience in the UK that the advice given is sound and works. The process of preparing the case and getting it down in writing is itself a confidence-building experience. Many families report that *making the decision* turns out to be the most difficult thing. Preparing the case and then getting their programme operational turns out to be much more straightforward than they could ever have believed.

In the next section, there is further practical advice from home-schoolers as to how they set about their programmes, whether structured which means pre-planned, unstructured - which really means emergent structures based on exploration, since no learning is unstructured - or a mixture of the two approaches. This leads into some ideas about the principles of living with children in the regular and intense way that home-schooling requires.

Anticipating the work of Alice Miller in books like *For Your Own Good (1987)*, Holt proposes that one of the most deep-rooted of the causes of our present problems is the way we treat children. The reactionary and the romantic views of children are both firmly rejected. One approach says we should 'force the badness out of them' or exercise some other version of 'tough love', the other says we should not influence them because this 'squeezes the natural goodness out of them'. Holt advocates an approach based on reasoning as better than either of these ideas. In my own experience of teaching and parenting, I have to say he is entirely vindicated in his approach.

Lifeschool

Home-based educators have the opportunity to pursue real learning in the real world, or 'lifeschool'. This is an advantage over almost all schools for, even in 'free' or alternative schools there is too much tendency to defer to what conventional schools do by taking learners away from the great richness and variety of the real world and replacing it with an artificial and contrived learning environment. As one parent puts it:

> *"Susan lives in a world of marvellous abundance; her resources are unlimited. She has not been 'socialised' by school to think that education is a supply of scarce knowledge to be competed for by hungry, controlled children." (p.169)*

Another family stresses the incidental learning of everyday events. They planned a special 'educational' field trip once a week as part of their learning programme. These were fun and not without value but the phoniness finally got to the family and they stopped doing it as a routine. The weekly trips to the town to shop, use the library, the bank, the post office and other local facilities were more valued as a result.

This leads Holt on to suggest that the country club remodelled as a family club would be a better expenditure of public money than schools. There would be no curriculum, just facilities and opportunities for meeting, living and doing things. The only school that operates like this appears to be Sudbury Valley School, USA. ᐱAs one parent observes, any young person who has been to the usual type of school knows that school is only a euphemism for a children's jail.

Ten pages of the book are given over to establishing the idea that play is serious for learners, in particular it is young children's work. Included are several accounts from families relating to this theme. This leads into one of John Holt's main themes, that of learning without teaching. Learning is defined in a quite straightforward way as 'finding out'. It may wound us a little to realise children can often get along very well as learners without adult help and that if they need it, they will ask for it.

He refers back to his proposition in *How Children Fail* that it was fear, boredom and the confusion of having constantly to manipulate meaningless words and symbols, that made children stupid, and adds a further insight:

> *"I now see that it was that, but far more than that, the fact that* ***others had taken control of their minds***. *It was being* taught, *in the sense of being trained like circus animals to do tricks on demand, that had made them stupid (at least in school) ... The most important question any thinking creature can ask itself is, 'What is worth thinking about?' When we deny its right to decide for itself, when we try to control what it must attend to and think about, we make it less observant, resourceful, and adaptive, in a word, less intelligent, in a blunter word, more stupid." (p.231)*

Learning difficulties

Dyslexia and problems with left and right identification are two of the learning difficulties explored in the next fifteen pages. Holt's experience as a teacher and his reflections on that experience lead him to argue that learning difficulties are usually created by the school. Parents,

> *"... should be extremely sceptical of anything the school and their specialists may say about their children and their condition and*

needs. Above all, they should understand that it is almost certainly the school itself and all its tensions and anxieties that are causing these difficulties, and that the best treatment for them will probably be to take the child out of school altogether." (p.233)

Children and work

A job is something you do for money. A career is a ladder of jobs. Work is something worth doing for its own sake which you might do for money or even if the work did not pay. Few young people give a hopeful, positive or enthusiastic response to the last one. They can only envisage a job. This limited vision that their society has given them then increasingly dominates learning as students grow older, for John Holt finds that the key question they ask is *"What do you have to do to pass the course?"* This is closely linked to the assumption that a job may result from the course. Enjoyment and satisfaction frequently have nothing to do with it:

"A young woman about to graduate from a school of education once said to me, 'Well, I've learned two things here, anyway - that I don't like children and I don't like teaching.' I asked why she went on with it. She said, 'I have to, I've spent too much time and money learning to do this, I can't turn around and start to learn to do something else'." (p.254)

Home-based education gives a chance to break with this negative view of jobs and work and the related attitude to learning, and do something more optimistic.

The findings of the Courts and legal strategies

The next fifty pages are devoted to home-schooling and the courts in the USA. Although the detail findings are specific to USA law, the general findings are of interest:

1. Parents have a right to educate their children in whatever way they believe in; the state cannot impose on all parents any kind of educational monopoly, of schools, methods or aims.

2. The state may not deprive parents of this right for arbitrary reasons, but only for serious educational ones, which it must make known to parents, with all the forms of due process.

3. A state that would deny parents these rights by saying that their home education plan is inadequate has a burden of proof to show beyond reasonable doubt that this is so. Parents are assumed to be competent to teach their children until proved otherwise.

4. In order to show that the parents' educational plans are inadequate, the state must show that its own requirements and regulations are educationally necessary and do in fact produce, in its own schools, better results that the parents get or are likely to get. On page 305, Holt gives a list of questions about what schools are doing and achieving that would make this difficult to prove.

Holt advises parents to resist an attempt to have their children measured by standardised tests. Making small concessions about the curriculum may be tolerated for the sake of harmony, but no concessions should be made over tests for these reasons:

> "(1) Even in the narrow area which they cover, the tests do not
> measure well what they claim to measure; (2) the tests do not
> touch those many areas outside the narrow school curriculum in
> which children may be learning a great deal. (p.302)

Advice to schools

The final part of the book is directed to schools and how they should respond to the growing home-schooling movement. The first recommendation is not to panic, for even with full school co-operation and support, Holt estimates that the number of home-schooled is not likely to exceed 10% of the schooled population. Most school-age children are likely to continue in schools, hopefully reformed to become more educational and less custodial. There are simply not enough parents who either like or trust their children enough for it to be otherwise. It is not just attendance laws that keep children in schools. The adult population in general wants it that way - it wants them out of the way during the daytime.

The main reason schools should co-operate with home-schooling is that of research by learning from the experience of the families and how they get such good results.

> "Home schoolers will not teach the schools what they so yearn to
> know, the one best way to do anything. What they will teach is
> that there is no one best way, and that it is a waste of time and

*energy to look for it; that children (like adults) learn in a great
many different ways; that each child learns best in the ways that
most interest, excite, and satisfy her or him; and that the business
of the school should be to offer the widest possible range of
choices, both in what to learn and ways to learn it. (p.331)*

Schools lack good feedback and homes can provide some. Home-schooled
children who come to school on a flexi-time basis will bring with them many
ideas, skills, activities, and resources to share with other children. In doing
this, Holt predicts, they will make the school a different, nicer and more
interesting place. Few people at present see schools as places they would go to
by choice.

*"Very few people now feel that way. Even when most people still
supported the schools in principle, hundreds of parents, many of
whom had even been good students, were telling or writing me
that most of their worst anxiety dreams were still school dreams,
or that every time they went into children's school, for whatever
reason, they could feel their insides tighten up and their hands
begin to sweat. Many kinds of places - concert halls, baseball
parks, theatres, parks, beaches, to name but a few - make most
people feel good as soon as they step into them. They think that
something pleasant, interesting, exciting is about to happen. For
their very survival, schools* need *people who feel that way about
them ..." (p.338)*

As regards teacher education, Holt proposes that a spell working with a home-
schooling family would be very stimulating for students and teachers who
choose it. I can verify that when I did this with my students at Birmingham, it
was of enormous benefit to both parties.

For his final comments John Holt emphasises that home-schooling is a
misnomer for it is not a school at all but a place of natural learning, a place of
home-based education. Schools need to move in this direction:

*"What I am trying to say, in short, is that our chief educational
problem is not to find a way to make homes* more *like schools. If
anything, it is to make schools* less *like schools." (p.347)*

Learning All the Time

Early in 1982, John Holt began work on what was to be his final book. Developing his interest and support for parents opting to educate that he had demonstrated in *Teach Your Own*, the book was to be about how children learn to read and write and count at home, with very little or no teaching. By the Spring of 1983, he had established clearly the purpose of the new book:

> *"The book will be a demonstration that children, without being coerced or manipulated, or being put in exotic, specially prepared environments, or having their thinking planned and ordered for them, can, will, and do pick up from the world around them important information about what we call the Basics.*
>
> *"It will also demonstrate that 'ordinary' people, without special training and often without large amounts of schooling themselves, can give their children whatever slight assistance may be needed to help them in their exploration of the world, and that to do this task requires no more than a little tact, patience, attention, and readily available information." (p.xv)*

He died in September 1985 with his final book drafted but not finally edited. His colleagues at Holt Associates took on the task of editing and publishing the book, guided by the instructions they had received from John. Because he had given such clear instructions and had written the bulk of it already, it was possible to assemble the book and be confident that it was close to what John had intended. The few gaps were filled by editing in other articles and pieces he had written, but the main activity was to be editing down the wealth of material. John had anticipated this: *"cutting and squeezing, not puffing up, is going to be the task."*

The publishers acknowledged the skill of Holt Associates and others in preparing the manuscript:

> *"The publishers wish to thank Nancy Wallace and Susannah Sheffer for much thoughtful editorial assistance. We are also grateful to Pat Farenga, Donna Richoux, and all the staff of Holt Associates for considerable help in making this publication possible. Each of these close colleagues and friends of John*

*Holt's is involved in furthering his ideas and beliefs and helped
us shoulder the difficult responsibility of editing and publishing
a posthumous book." (p.xvii)*

In order that his purpose would not be misinterpreted, John wrote a long letter
in June 1984, which contained this key passage:

*"This is not a book about 'How to Help Your Child Succeed in
School'. It is a book about children learning. By learning I
mean making more sense of the world around them. (Let me try
this again.) Learning, to me, means making more sense of the
world around us, and being able to do more things in it.
Success in school means remembering the answers to teachers'
questions, getting clever about guessing what questions they
will ask, and how to fool them when you don't know the answers.
Years ago, even before my first book came out, I was for a time
tutoring an eighth grader, who was having some troubles in
school. One day she asked me, with great seriousness, 'How do
you learn about history?' Taking her question as seriously as
she meant it, I said, 'I think you may be asking me two
questions: one, how do I learn more about history, and two, how
do I get better grades in history class in school? The first thing
to understand is that these are completely different and
separate activities, having almost nothing to do with each other.
If you want to learn more about how to find out about what
things were like in the past, I can give you some hints about
that. And if you want to find out how to get better grades in
your History class, I can give you some hints about that. But
they will not be the same hints'. She understood and accepted
this, and asked me for both kinds of hints, which I gave her. In
this book I will for the most part be discussing the first of these
two questions - what sorts of things might we do to make various
aspects of the world more accessible, interesting, and
transparent to children." (p. xvii)*

In the six chapters that follow, the themes addressed are those of reading and
writing, numbers and arithmetic, music, advice for parents, the learning style
of young children, and a summary of the nature of learning. John Holt's style
of writing makes the material very accessible and parents, young teachers and
seasoned educationalists all find the messages clear and intelligible. Because

he stays close to experience most of the time, rarely deriving theory from theory, his ideas have immediate appeal.

Reading and writing

The chapter on reading and writing uses the familiar Holt technique of assembling observations and cases of children actually learning to read. From these he draws out his principles of learning to read. He notes how children learn best when they are comfortable and that sometimes this means close physical contact. As touching children becomes more frowned upon in schools, homes win out in providing this feature. But it is not only the probable absence of 'cosy physical contact' in classrooms that can inhibit learning to read, it is the public scrutiny of your performance that can have negative effects:

> "... whether you are a 'gifted' five-year-old or a terrified, illiterate twelve-year-old, trying to read something new is a dangerous adventure. You may make mistakes, or fail, and so feel disappointment or shame, or anger, or disgust. Just in order to get started on this adventure, most people need as much comfort, reassurance, and security as they can find. The typical classroom with other children ready to point out, correct, and even laugh at every mistake, and the teacher all too often (willingly or unwillingly) helping and urging them to do this, is the worst possible place to begin." (p.3)

The figure of thirty hours needed to learn to read is offered - provided the conditions are positive and not inhibiting. This figure was quoted by a Danish teacher, had cropped up again in adult literacy classes and had been put forward by the Brazilian Paulo Freire in his experience of teaching reading to illiterate peasant adults. Thirty hours is one school week and this is the true size of the task, Holt proposes. It is not a difficult task unless we make it so:

> "Learning to read is easy, and most children will do it more quickly and better and with more pleasure if they can do it themselves, untaught, untested, and helped only when and if they ask for help." (p.8)

Holt concedes that this view is not popular with the experts who make a living out of the teaching of reading; they have 'advocated a great many foolish things'. The idea of reading readiness is singled out for comment. Showing children lots of books made up of pictures and asking silly questions about them is a mistake. What children need to get ready for reading, Holt argues, is exposure to a lot of print - not pictures, but print. The process is akin to that of learning to talk when children were surrounded by talk; they began to identify patterns in the jumble of sounds around them and take possession of some of the words.

> *"They need to bathe their eyes in print, as when smaller they bathe their ears in talk. After a while, as they look at more and more print, these meaningless forms, curves, and squiggles begin to steady down, take shape, become recognisable, so that the children, without yet knowing what letters and words are, begin to see, as I once did myself, after looking at a page of print in an Indian typeface, that this letter appears here, and that group of letters appears there, and again here. When they've learned to see the letters and words, they are ready to ask themselves questions about what they mean and what they say." (p.12)*

This exposure to lots of print can take many forms. The large print edition of the New York Times is recommended for USA parents and teachers. Other print material from the adult world can be assembled - official forms, timetables, newspapers, magazines, instruction manuals, leaflets, handbills, telephone directories especially yellow pages directories, road maps, letters and posters. Dictionaries, on the other hand, are over-rated since most people get big vocabularies by working out the meanings from the context and not by consulting dictionaries. In his lifetime, Holt reckoned, he had consulted dictionaries only about fifty times in total.

> *"The trouble with telling children what words mean, or asking them to ask the dictionary to tell them, is that they don't get a chance to figure out the meaning of the word. Figuring out what you don't know or aren't sure of is the greatest intellectual skill of all." (p.20)*

Next, we are moved on to look at the issue of phonics. Holt is in favour of 'sensible phonics' but identifies most of the phonics cult as nonsense that just gets in the way of successful reading. One reading expert identified 500 reading skills, later reduced to 273. Holt proposes that there are only two general ideas that need to be grasped and they are firstly, that written letters stand for spoken sounds, and secondly, that the order of the letters on the page, from our left to our right, corresponds to the order in time of the spoken sounds. Children do not need to recite these rules, only to know how to apply them. In addition:

> *"Aside from that, what children have to learn are the connections between the 45 or so sounds that make up spoken English and the 380 or so letters or combinations of letters that represent these sounds in written English. This is not a large or a hard task. But, as in everything else, the schools do a great deal to make it larger and harder."* (p.23)

The first mistake is to teach the sounds of each individual letter. This is false information especially in the case of consonants where only six or seven can be said by themselves, with four borderline cases, and the rest have a sound only if combined with a vowel in a word or syllable. Vowels have variable sounds depending on which consonants or combination of consonants they are associated with, so teaching these as sounds in isolation is also foolish. In addition, the actual definition of what counts as a vowel and a consonant is inconsistent.

The reading books used in schools are identified as a major obstacle to learning to read:

> *"The books that most children are compelled to learn to read from are beyond belief boring, stupid, shallow, misleading, dishonest, and unreal."* (p.28)

In his tribute to Holt, George Dennison says that John was never unkind to his opponents. This has always worried me since it puts intolerable burdens on the rest of us trying to continue the tradition of constructive doubt, and the questioning of the dogmas of schooling in particular and education in general. It is hard to feel kindly disposed to people who do so much damage by flouting both reason and evidence. So, it is with some relief that I find that he does not disguise his scorn in this instance, at least.

Some interesting statistics are introduced to make the point about reading books. In 1920, the readers available contained an average of 645 words. This number was reduced to 460 in the 1930s, to 350 in the 1940s and in the 1960s to between 113 and 173. The explanation offered is that as the readers became more and more boring, children learned to read less and less well. Children had a harder time working up an interest in this stuff and therefore in learning to read. The experts, however, concluded that the books were too difficult for children rather than too boring to hold their interest, and so set to make them easier - and made them more boring than ever.

The other mistake that schools make is identified as making children read aloud in class. This inhibits the natural process of self-correction of mistakes. This occurs in private reading with a sympathetic adult or other child, and in silent reading. But reading out loud in class puts a premium on getting in right first time or suffering the consequences of public exposure, amusement or worse. In this matter, Holt returns to the theme of his first book on how children learn to fail in the relatively learning-hostile arena of the classroom.

In learning to read, another obstacle put in the way of children is the pretence that the language conventions are self-evident and reasonable when, in fact, they are often arbitrary and inconsistent:

> *"In fact, there is nothing self-evident or natural or reasonable about it at all. We just do it that way. But nothing makes school more mysterious, meaningless, baffling, and terrifying to a child than constantly hearing adults tell him things as if they were simple, self-evident, natural, and logical, when in fact they are quite the reverse - arbitrary, contradictory, obscure, and often absurd, flying in the face of a child's common sense."*
> *(p. 32)*

> *"In a short section on spelling, there is a number of practical suggestions about how accurate spelling might be encouraged, but they are all linked to the proposition that the best way to spell better is to read a lot and write a lot.*

> *"People who spell badly - I have taught many of them - are not much helped by rules and drills. In all my work as a teacher, nothing I ever did to help bad spellers was as effective as not doing anything, except telling them to stop worrying about it, and to get on with their reading and writing."* *(p.36)*

As regards handwriting, Holt questions the whole notion of cursive handwriting, seeing it as something of a superstition. He found to his surprise, that the students in his classes who wrote most quickly and legibly used manuscript printing. He proved to himself in some experiments in his classes, that print was more legible and also faster. So where did the idea of joining up writing come from? It appears to persist purely out of a bad habit. John Holt decided to drop cursive writing from his own set of habits and taught himself manuscript printing instead. As far as he could tell, cursive writing evolved from an elaborate script invented for the slow process of engraving in copper. Some people, somewhere, decided to impose this style on children and so we are stuck with a bad idea. In the real world of typing, word-processing and printing, of course, such a silly idea is ignored. (Nobody is yet daft enough to impose joined-up figures in arithmetic on children, but give it time...)

At home with numbers

This section begins with the mischievous suggestion that if arithmetic were illegal, children would probably learn it and learn it better. Since so many adults have trouble with numbers, something must go wrong quite early on. Holt suggests that abstraction is introduced too soon and too often. Although numbers are abstract, they are abstractions of something and without that something, meaninglessness can soon follow.

> *"For this reason, it seems to me extremely important that children not be taught to count number names in the absence of real objects ... or put it differently, when little children first meet numbers they should always meet them as adjectives not nouns. It should not at first be 'three', or 'seven', all by itself, but always 'two coins', or 'three matches', or 'four spoons', or whatever it may be." (p.47)*

Children can be confused by isolated number facts, he continues, and four different ways of looking at the same fact should not be taught as if they were four unrelated facts. Thus, $2 + 3 = 5$, $3 + 2 = 5$, $5 - 2 = 3$, and $5 - 3 = 2$ are one number fact looked at in four different ways. The one fact can be expressed as ***** = *** **.

Once children have discovered this set of relationships they can discover the same things about any number. Since discovering for ourselves is more powerful than being told and then memorising, and in any case is more fun, learning is more efficient.

This section continues with John Holt giving a range of practical ways of helping children get confident with numbers. There is the 'home-made adding machine' and various grid games for learning tables. There are ideas on learning to multiply large numbers and how to cope with fractions.

He talks about 'bootleg maths' - the world of puzzles children try on each other furtively, and thus returns to his joke that if maths were illegal, children would learn it better.

In 'family economics' he suggests that children should know, or be able to know, about the finances of their families. This is introducing numbers and arithmetic in a real context which leads on to ideas such as interest, loans, percentages, instalments, mortgages, and insurance.

In his section on solving problems, his approach to learning maths becomes clear. Maths should be seen as fascinating and beautiful; it also has a few practical uses in solving some everyday problems. Above all, he argues, it should be *fun*. In meetings of teachers he always met those who angrily disagreed with this idea:

> "... *it often happens that someone says, usually in an angry tone of voice, 'Learning can't be all fun!' (what they usually mean by this is 'Learning can't ever be fun, or it isn't really learning'.) They are so wrong about this. Figuring things out, solving problems, is about as much fun as anything we human beings know how to do. For pleasure and excitement, hardly anything beats it, and few things come close."* (p.83)

Young children as research scientists

In this short section Holt moves on to the central theme of his work about how children learn. He sees them as born learners who turn experience into knowledge by the same methods as research scientists. They observe their surroundings, they speculate and wonder, and they ask themselves questions. They formulate possible answers, make theories, hypothesise and test out their ideas in various ways. Insensitive adults can and do eradicate this natural learning especially in the kind of schools we have established.

> "*If we attempt to control, manipulate, or divert this process, we disturb it. If we continue this long enough, the process stops. The independent scientist in the child disappears."* (p. 95)

Loving music

As a musician himself, and one who learned the cello late in his life, in his 50s, John Holt has decided views about learning music. His experience led him to question many of the dogmas about musical education. The first one he questions is this: if you do not start early, it is too late. Not only did this contradict his own personal experience in becoming a competent cello player in his 50s, he recalls how a manager of a professional class civic orchestra confirmed that many of the musicians she worked with were late starters, who did not begin until well into their twenties and later. The myth of 'if you do not start early, you might as well not start at all' operates as a self-fulfilling prophecy because the music institutions often base their activity on that assumption.

A second notion that Holt questions is that of the 'need to practice'. Why talk about practice at all? Why not just talk about playing the instrument? For professional musicians, the matter is clear, for playing for an audience is 'playing' and preparing to play for an audience is 'practice', but for amateurs the distinction is not valid. Amateurs just play their instruments either by themselves or with others. If they do not enjoy it the point of doing it is lost.

> *"We need to take serious account of the fact, well known to most musicians, that most children who have been to any great degree pushed into music, however skilful they may become at it, do not enjoy it very much. A number of my professional musician friends have said wistfully that they wished they loved music as much as I do." (p. 113)*

The next section looks at the work of Suzuki in Japan as well as some of the distortions of his ideas. The method appeals to Holt because it relies on the same approach as the one children used to learn their native language. Parents were to play recordings at home as often as possible, recordings of expert violinists playing the simple violin tunes so that children would get to know them. When the child was three, one of the parents would start violin lessons, taking the child with them. If, in due course the child showed interest in playing too, a child-sized violin would be produced so that they could join in. Later, they could have the opportunity to join other children who had learned the same tunes and, in due course, be introduced to musical notation, having learned to play by ear until then.

> *"... when a group of these children came to the New England Conservatory on a tour of the US, I was there to hear them, along with several hundred others, many of them music teachers. The children, perhaps twenty of them, came on-stage, healthy, energetic, and happy. At the time I thought the average age of the children might be five or six; I now think*

they may have been a year or two older. Dr. Suzuki and a young assistant checked the tuning of the children's violins. We waited in great suspense. What would they play? Perhaps some of the slower and easier tunes of Vivaldi, Handel, or Bach? Dr Suzuki gave the downbeat, and then away they went - playing not some easy tune but the Bach Double Concerto, in perfect time, tempo and rhythm, and with great energy and musicality. It was breathtaking, hair-raising. I could not have been more astonished if the children had floated up to the ceiling. Rarely in my life have I seen or heard anything so far beyond the bounds of what I would have thought possible." (p.115-6)

Sadly, Holt observes, the Suzuki method had become rigid in the hands of traditional music teachers who failed to understand the logistics of the approach. The exploration, discovery, adventure, joy and excitement of the original Suzuki approach had once again been slowly strangled and then replaced by formal and rigid instruction. This compulsion and rigidity has a price, he argues, for it does for Beethoven and Mozart what schools already do to Shakespeare.

What parents can do

The four-year-old John Holt and his sister used to slip out of bed, settle down at the top of the stairs to listen to the adult conversations going on below. He notes that young children learn so much from adult conversation. The one clear advantage the adults have is that they have been around longer and therefore have more experience and have some mental maps of the world around them. The *way* that they make that experience available is crucial:

"What adults can do for children is to make more and more of that world and the people in it accessible and transparent to them. The key word is access: *to people, places, experiences, the places where we work, other places we go - cities, countries, streets, buildings. We can also make available tools, books, records, toys, and other resources."* (p. 127)

Parents can help by answering questions honestly but avoiding the trap of using every question as an excuse to do some teaching. Answer the question and leave it at that, for if more information is needed, it will be requested. The child who was assigned to read a book on penguins in school wrote in his report that the book said more about penguins than he wanted to know. We must be aware of the dangers of penguinising, says Holt. He gives a further illustration of the child who exhausted her mother's knowledge and was advised to ask her father. The child replied, *"Well, I don't want to know that much about it."* A radical lesson is drawn from all this:

> *"Not only is it the case that uninvited teaching does not make learning, but - and this was even harder for me to learn - for the most part such teaching prevents learning. Now that's a real shocker. Ninety-nine percent of the time, teaching that has not been asked for will not result in learning, but will impede learning."* (p.128)

The reason is that uninvited teaching carries hidden messages. One is that you are not smart enough to see that this is important. Another is that you will probably not bother to find out unless I teach it to you. A third is that I need to teach you because it is difficult and you are not smart enough to sort it out for yourself. These are messages of distrust and even contempt. The problem is that we *like* teaching:

> *"We're a teaching animal, as well as a learning animal."*
> (p.129)

But we have to restrain that impulse and the need to explain things to everybody ... until we are asked. Even then, we have to answer sparingly and sensitively.

People who do not see this are often the same people who want 'more structure' to get them learning. This usually means some adult telling children what to do and how to do it. Only the structure of the task is legitimate, Holt proposes, not the will of the adult. To get the sense of the process by which good work is done, they need to watch adults or others and to learn by the power of example. Cooking, typing, drawing, gardening, woodworking, car maintenance are all everyday example of the opportunity to learn about structure. Workplaces are particular places that Holt wants to see opened up to children to gain these kind of experiences.

For the rest of this section, John Holt seems to begin to do the task I set myself in writing this book, for he begins to draw in ideas from several of his books to advise readers on how to help their children learn. The close and sympathetic observation of children is stressed and the need to go with the flow of children's learning. If we interfere with their styles of learning, it is likely to be counter-productive and lead to the self-defeating behaviours he described in *How Children Fail.* In *How Children Learn* and again in *Teach Your Own,* he had warned about the over anxious correction of mistakes which destroys the slower but more effective self-correcting processes. We fool ourselves if we think corrections are not received as reproofs and therefore lead to the weakening of confidence.

> *"It is always, without exception, better for a child to figure out something on his own than to be told - provided, of course, as in the matter of running across the street, that his life is not endangered in the learning. But in matters intellectual, I admit no exception to this rule. In the first place, what he figures out, he remembers better. In the second place, and far more important, every time he figures something out, he gains in confidence in his ability to figure things out." (p. 138)*

Next, Holt asks the question, 'How much praise do children need?' A little goes a long way, is his answer because too much praise creates 'praise junkies'. Children who get too much praise become dependent on continued adult approval and eventually frightened to make mistakes. The trouble with any external motivation is that it displaces or submerges internal motivation. If we praise them for everything they do that pleases us, they will learn to do things just to please us rather than for their own satisfaction, and then get worried about not pleasing us.

> *"What children want and need from us is thoughtful attention. They want us to notice them and pay some kind of attention to what they do, to take them seriously, to trust and respect them as human beings. They want courtesy and politeness, but they don't need much praise." (p. 140-1)*

But adults need not hold back from making suggestions, provided that it is clear it is a suggestion and that the child is free to reject it. Adults must learn to take 'no' for an answer to some and may be quite a lot of their endless stream of helpful suggestions.

The nature of learning

In his final chapter, John Holt starts with three misleading metaphors about education. The first is the idea that education is an assembly line in a bottling plant. Pupils are seen as empty containers coming down the conveyor belt. The teachers are stationed along the assembly line at intervals and squirt various amount of different subjects over the containers as they pass on during their 15,000 hour journey down the conveyor belt. The management decides what substances and in what quantities are to be squirted, how much at a time, and what is to be done about those containers that do fill up sufficiently.

The question of why so many of the containers leave the long journey down the conveyor belt more or less empty, or leak out their contents soon after leaving the factory, is not seriously addressed because of the persistent belief that squirting actually works i.e. that teaching, seen as squirting adult imposed knowledge at pupils, actually produces learning.

> *"If students don't know enough, we insist, it is because we didn't start squirting soon enough (start them at four) or didn't squirt the right stuff, or enough of it (toughen up the curriculum)."*
> *(p. 149)*

The second metaphor sees students as laboratory rats in a cage, being trained to do some kind of trick, usually of the kind they would not perform in real life. If the rat presses the right levers they are rewarded by a morsel of food, if not they get punishment in the form of an electric shock. The sequence is task-morsel or shock, or task-carrot or stick or task-positive reinforcement or negative reinforcement.

> *"The positive reinforcements in schools are teachers' smiles, gold stars, 'A's on report cards, dean's lists, and entrance into prestigious colleges, good jobs, interesting work, money and success. The negative reinforcements are angry scoldings, sarcasm, contempt, humiliation, shame, the derisive laughter of other children, the threats of failure, of being held back, of flunking out of school. ... at the end of this line are entrance to low-rank colleges or none at all, bad jobs or none at all, dull work if any, not much money or outright poverty." (p.150)*

The third metaphor is that of school as a mental hospital, a treatment institution. If the children do not learn what is presented, they are lazy, disorganised or mentally disturbed. They may have 'learning disabilities' or 'perceptual handicaps' or 'school phobia' or something. This kind of explanation is popular because it gets everybody off the hook. Anxious middle class parents can be reassured that they did nothing wrong, it is just that their child has some wires crossed in its head. Demands for schools to do better can be set aside with explanations about the numbers of the 'learning disabled' in the school.

> *"The 'research' behind these labels is biased and not very persuasive. Some years ago, at a large conference of specialists in learning disability, I asked whether anyone had heard of - not done, but merely heard of - any research linking so-called perceptual handicaps with stress. In the audience of about 1,100, two hands were raised. One man told me then, the other told me later, about research that showed that when students with supposedly severe learning disabilities were put in a relatively stress-free situation, their disabilities soon vanished."* (p.151)

All these metaphors distract us from the truth that children are natural learners who get better and better at it unless adults start preventing them from doing so. Such adults may have good intentions but bad understanding. They do not understand about natural learning. Learning, like breathing, is not an act of volition for children. They do not think 'Now I shall set to and learn this'. It is their nature to look about them, to take the world in with their senses, and to make sense out of it, without knowing that they are doing it or how they are doing it. Holt concludes that the idea that we can teach young children how to learn is utterly absurd.

> *"Children are not only extremely good at learning; they are much better at it than we are. As a teacher, it took me a long time to find this out. I was an ingenious and resourceful teacher, clever about thinking up lesson plans and demonstrations and motivating devices and all of that acamaracus. And I only very slowly and painfully - believe me, painfully - learned that when I started teaching less, the children started learning more.*

> *"I can sum up in five to seven words what I eventually learned as a teacher. The seven word version is: Learning is not the product of teaching. The five word version is: Teaching does not make learning ... organised education operates on the assumption that children learn only when and only what and only because we teach them. This is not true. It is very close to one hundred percent false."* (p. 160)

Adults may think they are introducing efficiency into children's natural methods of learning, but usually slow it down and then eliminate it. They then replace it with something that clearly does not work .

> *"What is efficient? How does a small child learn language? She absorbs with her ears an enormous amount of verbal information - if she is living in a family where she hears a lot of talk and where people talk to her.   Most of it she doesn't remember or doesn't even understand. But she picks out a bit here, a bit there. She picks out the things she wants and needs. We say, 'Ha, this is inefficient.   When we get her in school, we're going to show her the efficient way to study language.' We have grammar, our tenses, vocabulary lists.   But which is more efficient? Who learn languages better?" (p.154)*

John Holt wanted to rescue learning from the myth-makers. He proposed that:

> *"In short, what we need to know to help children learn is not obscure, technical, or complicated, and the materials we can use to help them lie ready at hand all around us." (p.162)*

Conclusion:

John Holt's 'principles for the reconstruction of learning'

When I wrote the first edition of this book, I had been working on some principles of educational reconstruction myself. This gave me the idea that it might be useful as a conclusion to this book on John Holt's ideas, to assemble from his writings a list of his likely principles for the reconstruction of learning By coincidence, I have been reworking the idea of principles of educational reconstruction prompted by a friend, just before working on the second edition of this book. You may find it interesting and instructive to compile your own version. In the meantime, here are my revised suggestions:

1. We need an education that aims to produce people who have no wish to do harm:

"The fundamental educational problem of our time is to find ways to help children grow into adults who have no wish to do harm. We must recognise that traditional education, far from ever solving this problem, has never tried to solve it. Indeed, its efforts have, if anything, been in exactly the opposite direction. An important aim of traditional education has always been to make children into the kind of adults who were ready to hate and kill whomever their leaders might declare to be their enemies." (*The Underachieving School,* p. 98)

2. Education should be about producing freethinkers:

"What it all boils down to is, are we trying to raise sheep - timid, docile, easily driven or led - or free men? If what we want are sheep, our schools are perfect as they are. If what we want is free men, we'd better start making some big changes." (*The Underachieving School*, p.36)

3. Compulsory schooling degrades the learning experience, so learning should become invitational:

"So the valiant and resolute band of travellers I thought I was leading towards a much-hoped-for destination turned out instead to be much more like convicts in a chain gang, forced under threat of punishment to move along a rough path leading nobody knew where, and down which they could hardly see more than a few steps ahead. School feels like this to children: it is a place where they make you go and where they tell you to do things and where they try to make your life unpleasant if you don't do them or don't do them right."

(*How Children Fail*, p. 37)

and:

"The schools can be in the jail business or in the education business, but not in both. To the extent that they are in the one they cannot be in the other."

(The Underachieving School p. 64)

4. Traditional authoritarian education is increasingly obsolete:

"The case for traditional education seems to me much weaker than it has been, and is getting ever weaker, and the case for an education which will give a child primarily not knowledge and certainty but resourcefulness, flexibility, curiosity, skill in learning, readiness to unlearn - the case ... grows ever stronger." *(The Underachieving School* p. 155)

5. The practice of unquestioning obedience will lead us inevitably into the bully or pre-fascist mentality:

"If we want a country in which everyone has his place, slave to everyone above him, master to everyone below him; a country in which respect for and obedience to authority is the guiding rule of life; a country, in short, like Germany in the generation before Hitler - if this is what we want, we are on the right track ..." *(The Underachieving School* p. 114)

6. Real choice and real diversity are essential requirements of a reconstructed system of learning:

"Only when all parents, not just rich ones, have a truly free choice in education, when they can take their children out of a school they don't like and have a choice of many others to send them to, or the possibility of starting their own, or of educating their children outside of school altogether - only then will we teachers begin to stop being what most of us still are, and if we are honest know we are, which is jailers, baby-sitters, cops without uniforms, and begin to be professionals, freely exercising an important, valued, and honoured skill and art." *(What Do I Do Monday?* p. 265)

7. Uninvited teaching is of dubious value:

"Not only is it the case that uninvited teaching does not make learning, but - and this was even harder for me to learn - for the most part such teaching prevents learning." *(Learning All the Time,* p. 128)

8. Giving too much help even when invited may destroy motivation:

"...interfering very much in the play and learning of children often stops it altogether." (*Learning All the Time*, p. 143)

9. Healthy children are curious and eager to explore the world and do not have to be motivated, unless insensitive adults have already damaged or weakened this natural urge to learn:

"...children are passionately eager to make as much sense as they can of the world around them, they are extremely good at it, and do it as scientists do, by creating knowledge out of experience." (*Learning All the Time*, p. 95)

and,

"Children ... are acting like scientists all the time, which is to say looking, noticing, wondering, theorising, testing their theories, and changing them as often as they have to." (*Learning All the Time*, p. 134)

10. Effective learning is only rarely the product of imposed teaching:

"I was an ingenious and resourceful teacher, clever about thinking up lesson plans and demonstrations and motivating devices and all of that acamaracus. And I only very slowly and painfully - believe me painfully - learned that when I started teaching less, the children started learning more.

"I can sum up in five to seven words what I eventually learned as a teacher. The seven word version is: Learning is not the product of teaching. The five word version is: Teaching does not make learning. Organised education operates on the assumption that children learn only when, and only what, and only because we teach them. This is not true. It is very close to one hundred per cent false."

(*Learning All the Time*, p. 160)

and,

"What we can best learn from good teachers is how to teach ourselves better."

(*Never Too Late*, p.2)

11. Imposed testing subverts education:

"To me, it seems clear that the greater the threat posed by a test, the less it can measure, far less encourage learning. There are many reasons for this. One of the most obvious, and most important, is that whenever a student knows he is being judged by the results of tests, he turns his attention from the material to the tester. What is paramount is not the course or its meaning to the student, but whatever is in the tester's mind. Learning becomes less a search than a battle of wits. The tester, whoever he is, is no longer a guide and helper, but an enemy." (*The Underachieving School* p. 53)

12. How *we* learn best also applies to children:

"I believe we learn best when we, not others, are deciding what we are going to try to learn, and when, and how, and for what reasons or purposes; when we, not others, are in the end choosing people, materials, and experiences from which and with which we will be learning; when we, not others, are judging how easily or quickly or well we are learning, and when we have learned enough; and above all when we feel the wholeness and openness of the world around us, and our own freedom and power and competence in it."

(*What Do I Do Monday?* p.95)

13. Schools will not change society:

"The comfortable and pleasant and powerful places in society are *occupied*, and the people who are in those places are not going to move out of them and down in society just so that poor people can move up and in."

(*Freedom and Beyond*, p. 185)

14. Custodial-type schools cannot teach morality:

"To talk of using the schools to teach morality is a bad joke. We might as well talk of using the Army to teach pacifism. As Edgar Friedenberg has well put it, powerlessness corrupts. The schools, by taking the power to make choices from their students, corrupt them." (*Instead of Education*, p. 191)

15. Most of our current assumptions about adults planning schooling in order to work *on* children rather than *with* children, are just plain wrong:

"I don't believe in the curriculum, I don't believe in grades, I don't believe in teacher-judged learning. I believe in children learning with our assistance and encouragement the things they want to learn, when they want to learn them, how they want to learn them, why they want to learn them. This is what it seems to me education must now be about."

(*The Underachieving School* p. 146)

16. We can reconstruct learning if we want to:

"Schools are not a force of nature. People made them, thinking they would be useful; people can do away with them when they are no longer of any use."

(*Instead of Education*, p. 213)

Editions of the Books by John Holt quoted in this volume

How Children Fail (1969) Harmondsworth: Penguin Books

How Children Learn (1970) Harmondsworth: Penguin Books

What Do I Do Monday? (1970) New York: E.P.Dutton & Co

The Underachieving School (1971) Harmondsworth: Penguin Books

Freedom and Beyond (1972) New York: E.P.Dutton & Co

Escape From Childhood (1975) Harmondsworth: Penguin Books

Instead of Education (1977) Harmondsworth: Penguin Books

Teach Your Own (1981) Liss: Lighthouse Books

Learning All the Time (1991) Ticknall: Education Now
            and Liss: Lighthouse Books (joint publication)

Never Too Late (1992) Ticknall: Education Now
            and Liss: Lighthouse Books (joint publication)

Revised editions

Revised editions of both *How Children Fail* and *How Children Learn* were published by Penguin books in 1984. In them, John Holt adds passages that record his later reflections on his earlier work. Most of these ideas are found in his later books, as presented in this volume. I have not, therefore, produced any separate notes on these two revised works.